What's *Wrong* With Millennials?

Also by <u>Kevin</u> <u>Klix</u>:

FICTION

Biflocka
A Lion in Your Number
Elevator Music
Skateboy
The Student
Wasp in the Opium Flowers

NON-FICTION

Beautiful Nihilism

SELF-HELP

A Wellness Guide to Happiness
Stop Unreality

POETRY

*Why I F*cking Hate Poetry*

What's *Wrong* With Millennials?

Decoding the Forces That Shaped
a Generation's Way of Life

Kevin Klix

k Publishing Co. | Est. 2012

Dedicated to Millennials.

Obviously.

Table of Contents

What's *Wrong* With Millennials?

ACKNOWLEDGEMENTS

One thing is for certain, I will have to thank my girlfriend, Casey Milner-Knotts, for pushing me to keep writing down words and for always reading my essays, even though she did not have to. She is a saint and, dare I say, a "gem" in my eyes. And for that, she needs to be acknowledged.

My brother, Steven Klix, Jr., for obviously making me realize the direction in which my life is going and for making sure that I stick to writing even though it was against his personal ends. He once told me, while riding in his work van, "You need to write thousands of books to reach as many people as possible. Then you can make a career out of this thing." While I can't possibly write a thousand books, I understood his sentiment.

My mother and stepfather for kicking me in the ass when I needed it most, and for possibly shaping the way I am today. And also for giving me a perfect example of the generation before mine, whether they'd like to admit it or not.

As bad as I don't want to say it, I will have to thank the existence of Google for making this whole process of looking up stats specifically on Millennials easy-peasy, even though the stats and articles I would invariably have to look up for said corresponding subjects seemed to be heavily censored and curated.

"The Whatever Podcast" for inspiring me to come up with the idea as to why Millennials are so messed up. Every guest and every conversation on your guy's show baffled me and made me want to dive in and do my own research on the mindset of Millennials, the generation your show seems to highlight, consciously or unconsciously.

And I want to further expound on my generation, and how much I truly love all of you that are within it. I understand more than you know about the struggles, the benefits, and the overall mindset that we all seem to carry. I know because I lived it and carried it myself. To each their own, though. Everyone's life is different. Always take what I say with a grain of salt. But no matter, I still love and appreciate you all just the same. Kudos to you!

INTRODUCTION

Millennials. A dirty word to some. A liberating one to others. Well, sort of "liberating." It's an identity, a generation. It means a whole lot in many different ways to many different people. For better or for worse, depending on who you ask. For those born between the years of 1981 through 1996, the first one (maybe two) decades were both a golden age and an age where innocence was lost.

For those older than Millennials, it is no secret that there is a level of disdain for this mysteriously "entitled" generation, as coined by the *Times*, especially since 71% of American adults think of them this way[1]. And probably for good reason. The generation before cannot possibly foresee the struggles that their preceding generation can/will/is going through, according to a study that illustrates how each generation perceives and develops wisdom differently through shared learning environments.[2] But to be fair, I would assume that every generation before its predecessor always views itself to be harsher and much more enriched with real wisdom and life experiences that it feels the generation after them lacks. And probably this is by virtue of things getting easier in life as humans discover and invent new ways of making our society easier to stomach.

To put it simply and as frankly as possible, I wanted to unpack why Millennials think, feel, and act the way they do, and how this potentially will shape and mold future generations (currently Generation Z, and afterward, Generation Alpha) into whatever they may become. Maybe this understanding and insight can better connect all older, current, and future generations and make them work together in harmony. God knows that we need that in our world's chaotic modern times. . . .

For my own selfish reasons, I want to get to the bottom of why this phenomenon of perceived "entitlement" and way of living/thinking is occurring within Millennials. Maybe in the process understand *myself* better. I have lived through the '90s as a small child, grew up with the inception of touch-screen smartphone technology, and saw the rise of the internet, social media, and mass communication systems. I seemingly have pieced together, little by little, where exactly this collective mindset that appears all Millennials have: This feeling of a dark future looming over us; this feeling of dread, skyrocketed mental health illnesses, coupled with crippling anxiety and self-absorbed affliction towards what the world, the country, and our lives hold. In much simpler terms, the Millennial mind longs for radical change towards a future utopic society that we feel is entirely (and hopefully) within our grasp —as long as everyone is on board with it, that is. . . . In a way, it is an insidious hive mind. It's no wonder there is obvious push-back, especially from the older generations.

The Millennial mind has left traditional roles by the wayside, according to a study that illustrates and explores how urban Millennial families are modifying their home spaces to suit their lifestyles, which often include remote work and hobbies. This study illustrates how Millennials are departing from conventional uses of living spaces to accommodate modern needs.[3] Sometimes through no fault of our own, and sometimes without our collective consent.

There is an itch for that perfect, soulmate-styled love and acceptance that we Millennials desire more than anything, but also completely do not care about in the slightest due to our pessimistic sense and nihilistic outlooks. While there are always spiritual, religious, and sometimes outlying Millennials out there, statistics show through Pew

Research studies ("Religion Among the Millennials")[4] that there is a sharp decline every generation in regards to denominations:

> By some key measures, Americans ages 18 to 29 are considerably less religious than older Americans. Fewer young adults belong to any particular faith than older people do today. They also are less likely to be affiliated than their parents' and grandparents' generations were when they were young. Fully one-in-four members of the Millennial generation – so-called because they were born after 1980 and began to come of age around the year 2000 – are unaffiliated with any particular faith. Indeed, Millennials are significantly more unaffiliated than members of Generation X were at a comparable point in their life cycle (20% in the late 1990s) and twice as unaffiliated as Baby Boomers were as young adults (13% in the late 1970s). Young adults also attend religious services less often than older Americans today. And compared with their elders today, fewer young people say that religion is very important in their lives.

But is this really that surprising? For those older than the Millennial generation, it baffles them that the values once held by religion and its doctrines have been thrown away and replaced with new ("moral") philosophies that have inevitably permeated into politics, corporate America, the media, and society as a whole. This radical change is extremely uncomfortable for these individuals, especially through the eyes of the traditional identity of religious dogma, and the possibility of it imploding. . . . Easily-accessible information, big and small, throughout the early 2000s has enlightened us into what it means to live within life and its many environments, so much so that the environments *themselves* feel as though they are not real, not purposeful, and—dare I say—quite godless. . . .

It's much easier to turn to science and technology as our new all-seeing "god," especially since now, through the click of a button, we can answer any and all philosophical, legal, moral, medical, spiritual, health and wellness questions to our heart's desire, and without so much as picking up any holy book. It has made a new mindset into the heart of what it means to be "good" and "just."

When the collective mind of social media and micro-blogging technology has connected us and brought together a massive coalition of individuals who all feel and think the same way, it's no wonder a hive-mind of so-called "entitlement" has formed. Experience has become a commodity within the Millennial generation. We simultaneously want equal livelihoods whilst also despising the current status quo of American living: the humdrum lifestyle of fancy cars, money, items, things, et cetera. (But secretly—and outwardly—we like it, too!) The Millennial generation is, admittedly, confused beyond all reason, and older generations cannot stand this.

Ultimately many of the issues associated with Millennials are teeming with undertones associated with lack of commitment. Do you blame them, though? In this fast-paced, instantaneous world, it makes it almost impossible to cling to and commit to literally anything. When technology makes everyone popular, every one a "god," everyone the same and enriched in all topics, it makes life boring—and in turn, it makes all things boring. The next fix, however—and the next big thing promised by tech companies—is always one click away. As long as you stay on their application. Hook, line, and sinker. The perfect psychological scam, in my mind.

One cannot discuss the Millennial generation without addressing the elephant in the room: Technology. At least, according to a paper that examines the influence of digital technology and organizational culture on behavioral innovation among Millennials, there is a significant emphasis on the critical role technology plays in shaping their professional behaviors and expectations.[5] This generation has been at the forefront of technological advances, from the early days of the internet to the omnipresence of smartphones. Millennials are considered digital natives, a term that signifies their innate familiarity with digital technology, which they have been exposed to from an early age. This familiarity has sculpted a unique worldview, distinguishing them from their predecessors. Social media, in particular, has redefined communication, enabling instant connectivity but also fostering a culture of comparison and immediate gratification. This digital landscape has significantly impacted Millennials' mental health and their perceptions of success and fulfillment.

The economic landscape has also uniquely shaped the Millennial experience. Many entered the job market during the 2008 financial crisis, an event that left deep scars on their economic prospects and attitudes toward money.[6] The dream of a stable job, a house, and a comfortable life, once a seemingly attainable milestone for previous generations, now appears a distant fantasy for many. Coupled with unprecedented levels of student loan debt,[7] these economic challenges have led to a sense of disillusionment and a reevaluation of traditional life milestones. The gig economy, with its promise of flexibility and entrepreneurship, has been both a symptom of these challenges and a desperately embraced solution.[8]

The reevaluation extends beyond economics into broader social norms and values. Marriage rates, for instance, have declined among Millennials,[9] reflecting changing attitudes towards personal commitment and the institution itself.[10] This shift accompanies a broader move away from traditional structures and norms, seen in everything from career paths to spiritual beliefs. The Millennial emphasis on personal growth, mental health, and inclusivity marks a significant cultural shift, one that prioritizes individual fulfillment over societal expectations.[11]

Finally, global events have profoundly influenced the Millennial psyche. From the shadow of 9/11 to the unprecedented challenges of the COVID-19 pandemic, Millennials have witnessed and navigated a rapidly changing world. These events have underscored the interconnectedness of global communities and the fragility of life, leading to a heightened sense of global responsibility and a call for change that spans from environmental action to social justice, despite significant backlash. In sum, the Millennial generation, often maligned and misunderstood, embodies a complex confluence of technological, economic, social, and global factors. Their unique experiences and challenges have fostered a distinct set of values and perspectives, influencing societal shifts and shaping the future landscape in profound ways.

Will the Millennial generation ever be both understood and accepted at the same time? I personally do not think so, at least not for a while—or maybe it'll be when it's too late and too irrelevant to care. I'm a pessimist in that respect. But I would like to blur the lines between that divide, at least in some way through the process of understanding. Do I want to play devil's advocate and defend Millennials? Yes, but I also want to play the same devil's advocate for the generation I am a part of, so we, too, can understand the other side of the story. I offer you, the reader, nothing more than that education and insight. I will do my best to make sure both sides are appeased.

But make no mistake, I do not plan to—or ever be—the mouthpiece of a generation. I am just a man who writes, researches, and has an itch for wonder. I want to first make American culture better; I want to bridge divisions within this country. But that does not mean I want to leave other countries besides America at the wayside, because, after all, Millennials come in all shapes and sizes, countries and creeds. Being as I was born and raised in America, and have seen the progression from the '90s to the mid-'20s, I have a unique and very different experience than most of the world—I surely know that.

I want the people of my generation—my *age*—to prosper and be healthy. We eventually are going to be prominent figures in society, just like Boomers took over their parents and their parent's parents. The circle of life is among us, and I want to unpack this generation I'm in and make sure it is understood and possibly prepare any and all that would want to learn about it.

I desire an understanding. I want intellectually sound arguments as to why a generation is the way it is, what is in store, and what may move us forward. And that is my only goal, my only *purpose*, and my (hopefully not only) reason for making and producing literature. Moving our lives forward should and always be the goal.

Who knows, maybe the right reader can take what I say and have the epiphany that we all need. But such a reader, firstly, has to understand and unpack themselves in a way that is cohesive, impactful, and constructive. This is what all of us *hope* for. This is what all generations *strive* for. And this, my friends, is the Millennial generation's time! :)

Footnotes:

[1] Gillespie, Nick. August 21st, 2014. "Millennials Are Selfish and Entitled, and Helicopter Parents Are to Blame". https://time.com/3154186/millennials-selfish-entitled-helicopter-parenting/

[2] DeMichelis, C., Ferrari, M., Rozin, T., & Stern, B. (2015). Teaching for Wisdom in an Intergenerational High-School-English Class. Educational Gerontology, 41, 551 - 566. https://doi.org/10.1080/03601277.2014.994355.

[3] Prabawa, M., & Gunawarman, A. (2020). A Study of The Ideal Home Space Needs of Urban Millennials Families, Based on Life Cycle Space (Case Study of Housing in East Denpasar). . https://doi.org/10.4108/eai.13-12-2019.2298274.

[4] Unknown Author [Report]. February 17th, 2010. "Religion Among the Millennials". http://pewrsr.ch/14gdPzX

[5] Nawangsari, L., & Sutawidjaya, A. (2020). "Does Organizational Culture and Digital Technology influence Behavioral Innovation in Millennial Generation?". https://doi.org/10.4108/eai.26-11-2019.2295156.

[6] Yang, J., Roman-Urrestarazu, A., & Brayne, C. (2018). Binge alcohol and substance use across birth cohorts and the global financial crisis in the United States. PLoS ONE, 13. https://doi.org/10.1371/journal.pone.0199741.

[7] Kern, S. (2016). "Falling Behind to Get Ahead: The Millennial Student Debt Trap?". ABA Banking Journal, 108, 30.

[8] Disha Singh. (2023). Theoretical Integration of Gig Economy: Exploring various Prospects, Challenges and Regulatory Measures. International Journal For Multidisciplinary Research. https://doi.org/10.36948/ijfmr.2023.v05i01.4860.

[9] Khan, K., Zubair, S., & Koseoglu, S. (2020). Are the Millennials Getting Less Married?. , 4, 76-90. https://doi.org/10.47264/IDEA.LASSIJ/4.1.8.

[10] Stark, M., Kirk, A., & Bruhn, R. (2012). Generational Differences as a Determinant of Women's Perspectives on Commitment. Adultspan Journal, 11, 112-122. https://doi.org/10.1002/J.2161-0029.2012.00010.X.

[11] Steffy, K. (2023). Habits of the Millennial Heart: Individualism and Commitment in the Lives of Young, Underemployed Americans. Sociological Focus, 56, 226 - 245. https://doi.org/10.1080/00380237.2023.2180465.

["the formation of identities": transgenderism, political affiliations, race, and occupations]

Our identities are highly important, not only to Millennials but to most everyone. It's what gives us unique perspectives, unique approaches, and unique lives. It's what gives flavor and color to life as we know it. Cultures themselves can have micro-identities within their social ecosystems. Perhaps it makes sense that if there are two alike humans in this world, it would crumble most philosophical standpoints and how we view what it means to be a human being. After all, even if you had two completely identical people together—even just a foot apart—that tiny amount of space between them would cause a rift in their respective perspectives and still inevitably make them different. Time and space cannot house two of the same beings at once. In other words, it's impossible by virtue of our conscious perspectives and lives to have two completely same individuals, even throughout the billions of them on this planet. And that's a fortunate thing.

It is hard to pinpoint exactly why it seems Millennials, in particular, are so hyper-infatuated with identity. Perhaps social media, the pursuit of internet viewership clout, trends that come and go (but in very drastic and powerful succession), research pertaining to health, wellness, and being the best individual you can strive to be—these things all seem to propel an already impressionable Millennial into a state of perpetual yearning for the next thing that will further make one unique and beautiful in this life that we all inhabit.[1] Though it seems unique-ness, unfortunately, has become a currency with which those in power (including those in politics, entertainment, and corporations) can weld as a manipulative tool towards individuals. There is a monetization of identity that we can only perceive to be possible due to the internet and its pupils. And it seems that Millennials are the first generation to really take the reins of that sentiment. You can prove that this is so, simply by looking at the data that suggests Millennials are more prone to wanting unique identities than the generations before and after them:

> Younger Americans are often assumed to be the most progressive when it comes to ideas about gender and sexuality. Gen-Z —aged 18 to 24—are more likely to identify as LGTBQ+, according to recent research.¶ Surveying more than 2,000 US adults across age groups, locations, and socioeconomic backgrounds, researchers found that Generation Y (25-39 years old) had the highest rates of opposition to the traditional gender binary.[2]

The LGBTQ+ community, in a sense, has turned into a bastion of *identity*, and Millennials have invested in it full swing. Uniqueness has turned into a yearning to go against the status quo, whatever that may be perceived, real or otherwise. It's no secret that Millennials have grown, as a whole, to be more left-leaning politically. According to *The Financial Times*[3], it appears that every generation prior to Millennials has typically always started in their early twenties as left-leaning, and then in their thirties they shift towards right-leaning principles. The trope comes to mind: "If you are not a liberal at 25, you have no heart. If you are not a conservative at 35, you have no brain." A dig towards

Millennials, rest assured. *The Financial Times*, furthermore, gave their own research and seemingly proved that Millennials, even as they age, do not seem to outgrow their liberal tendencies:

> If Millennials' liberal inclinations are merely a result of this age effect, then at age 35 they too should be around five points less conservative than the national average, and can be relied upon to gradually become more conservative. In fact, they're more like 15 points less conservative, and in both Britain and the US are by far the least conservative 35-year-olds in recorded history.

Coupled with a yearning for change and wanting to be unique, it is easy for the Millennial generation to turn to identity politics most prevalent within the Democratic Party. The status quo, according to said identity politics, is what is known as a *straight white male*. And it is compelling to make sense of it, by simply looking at United States history and how this demographic dominated every aspect of this country: financially, imperialistically, and through seemingly strong-arming any that they oppose, including those they would exploit (i.e., slavery). To put it simply, in the mind of those subscribed to this status quo's existence and its dominance, to be a *straight white male* is sacrilegious beyond all order.

To be black or gay or anything other than a *straight white male* is, therefore, considered virtuous. Progressive. Noble. Ideal. An identity with a like-minded community of people that can give them the same sense of *togetherness* and *love* that is almost akin to attending church on Sunday mornings. Right-wingers, therefore, opposed these doctrines and simply write them off as an apparent cult—or dogmatic corrosion. (Though left-wingers feel the same way towards them.) Regardless, even mundane and benign things like pronouns have been almost euphemistic for wanting a fortified identity. To be another pronoun is to put another notch into the individual's unique identity. Therefore, it is easy for a Millennial to subscribe to it.

Mainly, though, I'm discussing Western politics. On the Eastern side, countries like Pakistan, Iran, and even Ukraine have wildly different cultures and backgrounds, and therefore produce a wildly different type of Millennial. There are Millennials on that side of the planet exercising jihad, a struggle or fight against the enemies of Islam. Through any means necessary, even through outright violence or death. Currently, in 2024, there are Millennials in Ukraine fighting off a war with a Russian superpower. Clearly, there is a pampering (however perceived in comparison to the East) of Millennials in the West going on that needs to be addressed. Could it be that one reader reading these words in the West could be feeling wildly different than someone in the East? Maybe issues and struggles going on among Western Millennials pale in comparison to the issues and struggles of those in the East. Regardless of how many identities collide, it should be noted that everyone deals with countless varieties of trials-and-tribulations that shouldn't be discounted—though there are different levels and severities, obviously. It is easy for a person's shoes to look shiner, freer, and more robust than your own—and this, as a result, can make you feel a sense of *envy*.

Our phones are no help, either. Our smartphones and our algorithms lead us down a spiraling path towards envy. In my eyes, it appears that the very idea of clout, viewership, or popularity is predicated on envy: the more the content makes others envious, the higher you are on the social hierarchy of the internet. But the reality is that no two entities can simultaneously be number one; therefore, there must always be another that is playing second fiddle. Within the realm of social media, there is always a power struggle for clicks, likes, clout, and the acceptance of others. If you are relatively uninteresting, "average," or God forbid unacceptable to your peers, in the eyes of a social media junkie, an aspiring influencer (who are often Millennials and Gen-Zers), this appears to be the death of one's identity, according to those who subscribe to the idea. . . .

W here did they, the Millennial generation, go wrong with this hyper-infatuation with identity? Could it be the very fact that technology connecting us to every single person in the world has made the hypothetical pond of talent, identity, uniqueness, and popularity—the things most desired by Millennials—thinner and thinner?

It seems as though the true struggle with identity is having a specific feeling of success, a specific feeling of *togetherness*. Respect. Dignity. Embrace. It also appears as though power and money have become a hyper-facet of American life that has made its way into the minds of the young, the middle, and the old. And though it seems rather silly—and frankly laughable—that certain someones could so naively ask a question that seems obvious when talking about American culture, here I am asking it as directly as I can. Money and value, after all, have granted America the said title of superpower in this world—therefore, it would make sense that of all its time since its inception, the people within it would have an obsession with money, value, or anything that shoots your individual status sky-high.

But does money matter when we discuss identity? Money shouldn't even play that much of a role in who we are as people, right? This can be so, but . . . when our phones, televisions, and screens are all showing us the lives of people seemingly better and more well-off than us, the tools of money and lifestyle appear to overtake the conversation in our heads. When finding out what makes a person unique and all-special, money does seem to propel any and all possible abilities towards discovering what makes you you. Accessibility to resources, in other words, makes it easier to reveal your true identity.

This accessibility to resources is the backdrop to any viral influencer. Through the lens of an Instagram model, a successful musician, or a heartthrob comedian, there almost always is a thin inkling of a luxurious lifestyle attached to it. The success they are showcasing inevitably comes across to viewers as universal acceptance and love from those following them. This is why celebrity is so appealing. To go freely galavanting around the world and about town with your cell phone doing all types of adventures and epic memories appears to the average Millennial the highest form of success. But for an impressionable Millennial without these things—or who sees him- or herself as not having or never being about to have said things—it's easy for the inevitable envy to turn into hatred, unhealthy longing, rage, and even radicalism. These very emotions are the catalyst for leftist ideology. And I cannot say I blame them for reaching that conclusion.

At face value, Communist and Marxist ideology appears to be a perfect system. On paper, the ideal of true equality, true commune, and true sense of togetherness and ultimate sharing resembles that of a utopia. Things come to mind such as nobody being without basic needs, nobody having health issues because of how abundant medical care is, nobody having to struggle with any form of work due to all work being equally important, and any and everyone always and unquestionably helping one another out monetarily. Good fortune, goodwill, compassion, honesty, and graciousness are the backdrop of such a society. This is what is promised to an impressionable Millennial through left-wing politics and Marxist thought.

When push comes to shove, though, and you throw a Millennial out into the wild that is Life, the shell shock and reality of the situation is that we are very, very far from any kind of utopia. As a huge lover of America, I can safely say we are in the best possible situation for what we have living in the West, but we also have such a ways to go towards true progress. Everyone always has their spin on what they perceive as "progress." Hence, this is why Communism/Marxism falls flat: Human beings are inherently not equal. If a person is born tall and a person is born short, what comes with either of these people is advantages and disadvantages. Or someone born with mental health issues, or any issues for that matter. It's easy for one to consider that if someone is born in a situation that gives them an edge—like wealth, height, beauty, talent, a good, functioning mind, a powerful brain, you name it—they inevitably will gain privilege and therefore be unequal to those without those things. The problem with true equality is that two radically bad things happen: (a) You take a person who is lower in the hierarchy and place virtue on them when they may not give you the results you are after in whatever field or practice, or (b) Those that do have virtue and are "better" and with perspective merit have to be stripped in order to equalize the population. Both hinder progress. One makes it to where you can't do better because you will get something taken from you to equalize. The other gives power and merit to those who may not have the strength or wherewithal to handle the task.

This merit I speak of does not necessarily have to apply to Capitalism. It could be something as simple as placing someone in a position as a speaker to a group of people for a good, non-profit cause, but the person is skittish, shy, or is unable or unwilling to effectively speak to said group. This would collapse the cause and hinder progress. This is why you would put someone with speaking merit, for example, in that position. Though I do think in this example most would give the person the benefit of the doubt. People aren't stupid and can sense if someone is trying their best. Someone can become a good speaker through practice and gain merit. But there is always a catch-22 in all regards.

For a left-wing Millennial, it is very uncomfortable to come to terms with the concept of merit, because if it exists then it threatens the very goal of equality and Marxist thought. The only way to combat the concept is to use it against your opponent, spin it, and frame it through the lens of pity, guilt, or remorse. This is why it is so easy for a left-wing Millennial to use smear tactics such as racism, sexism, homophobia, et cetera, as a means to vilify those who believe in and know that merit exists. But it's so popular and so vastly promoted on social media, Hollywood, and the press, that it makes the average person want to be silent on the subject for fear of acknowledging it. This in turn makes it easy for them to frame equality as objective truth and an obtainable goal. An impressionable Millennial can easily fall victim to radical and all-encompassing hyper-racism that they perceive permeates through all facets of life through what they have been told and taught. . . . (It should be noted, though, that racism, sexism, homophobia, et cetera, are not to be taken lightly, and do actually exist. This adds an extra layer to the conversation as to what merit truly means. And if it holds objective truth. Both exist—equality and merit—but both cannot *coexist* in the minds of human beings, strictly because of their incompatibility.)

In this intricate dance of identity, equality, and merit, we find ourselves at a crossroads of ideals and realities. It's a tightrope walk between celebrating the uniqueness of each individual and advocating for a society that levels the playing field. One must grapple with the stark truth that while we yearn for a world where everyone's worth is measured on the same scale, we're ensnared in a reality where life deals a different hand to each of us. The challenge lies in mitigating these disparities without stifling the pursuit of excellence. Merit becomes a layered puzzle, not just an inherent trait, but a product of circumstances, opportunities, and support structures that prop individuals up. It's not merely about who you are, but also about the resources at your disposal (i.e., often the privileges you have been born into or are given).

In this delicate interplay of identity, merit, and equality, it's crucial to foster conversations that acknowledge the intricate tapestry of every person's journey. Recognizing privilege and leveraging it for the collective good can be a potent catalyst for change. Likewise, celebrating diverse achievements, whether born of natural talent or hard-fought effort, reinforces the idea that success takes many forms. For the left-leaning Millennial, reconciling the ideals of merit and equality demands a nuanced understanding of their coexistence. It's not about erasing distinctions, but about dismantling the systems that unfairly tip the scales in favor of a select few.

In the end, the road to a more equitable society is a collective endeavor. It calls for a commitment to dismantling the structures that perpetuate discrimination, amplifying voices that have been marginalized, and ensuring equal access to opportunities. It implores us to recognize that true progress lies in embracing the complexity of human experience and cherishing the contributions of every individual, regardless of the hand they've been dealt.

Reader's Group Discussion Questions

- How do you believe social media and the internet have influenced the Millennial generation's obsession with identity? Discuss the positive and negative impacts of this influence on personal development and societal perceptions.

- The chapter suggests that Millennials' political affiliations are closely tied to their identities, particularly in relation to progressive ideals and opposition to traditional norms. How do you see this relationship affecting political discourse and societal change?

- Considering the diverse experiences of Millennials globally, as highlighted through the contrasting situations in Western versus Eastern contexts, what insights does this offer about the universality of identity struggles? How do these differences inform our understanding of the Millennial generation as a whole?

- Discuss the concept of uniqueness being used as a currency by those in power, as mentioned in the chapter. How does this commodification affect individual authenticity and societal values?

- The chapter delves into the complex relationship between merit and equality, posing challenges to achieving true societal progress. How can we reconcile these concepts in a way that promotes fairness without disregarding individual achievements and circumstances?

- With the prevalence of envy and the pursuit of clout through social media, as discussed in the chapter, what strategies can individuals and communities adopt to foster healthier relationships with identity and success in the digital age?

Footnotes:

[1] 'Aisy, J., & Pandin, M. (2021). THE INFLUENCE OF SOCIAL MEDIA FOR YOUNG GENERATION; THE POTENTIAL TO DAMAGE THE NATIONAL IDENTITY. https://doi.org/10.31219/osf.io/mvx7r.

[2] LAndsverk, Gabby. February 27th, 2021. *Business Insider*. "Gen Zers are less progressive than Millennials about gender identity and stereotypes, a new survey says". https://www.insider.com/millennials-more-progressive-than-gen-z-about-gender-survey-finds-2021-2?amp

[3] Financial Times Staff. December 29th, 2022. *Financial Times*. "Millennials are shattering the oldest rule in politics". https://www.ft.com/content/c361e372-769e-45cd-a063-f5c0a7767cf4

[are we what we eat?: the possibility that our food consumption, our prescription drugs, our air, and our water have tainted us]

Ask any of your elders what the food was like back before it is currently, and they almost always will respond with, "It was better." When asking why, you will get a maundered of answers ranging from "the food used to not be processed," "the food used to not be product," and even "the food used to *taste* better!" Is any of this true? Does any of it hold merit? Could it be that the nostalgia of the past has tainted the present-day memory of their food consumption?

Once upon a time, the dinner table was a tableau of simplicity: locally sourced meats, vegetables straight from the garden, and fruit picked fresh from the tree. Today, the modern plate is a global affair, laden with processed foods, genetically modified organisms (GMOs), and a cocktail of nasty preservatives. The shift from farm-to-table to factory-to-table reflects broader societal changes, including urbanization and the rise of convenience as a commodity. This transformation has not been without consequence. The prevalence of diet-related diseases such as obesity and diabetes has surged, casting a shadow over the Millennial generation's health landscape. Beyond physical health, the industrialization of food production has ushered in a cultural shift, where meals are no longer just about sustenance but identity and lifestyle choices, influenced heavily by marketing and the digital age's omnipresence.

When we talk about food and marketing, "buzzwords" in food come to mind. Things like: Natural. Organic. Gluten-Free. Sugar-Free. Reduced-Sugar. Fat-Free. So on and so forth. When you are discussing such buzzwords, it's easy to forget that these companies are, in fact, corporations; corporations, mind you, that *want* and *need* to turn a profit—oftentimes a *huge* profit, even at the expense of other's health. This means that even though they use these buzzwords, they aren't always as honest as they should be. If there was ever a grey area of truth, it most certainly would be within the food industry. "Gluten Free" could mean it's without gluten, but it could also have traces of gluten that fall just below regulatory thresholds imposed by the Food & Drug Administration (FDA), yet could still affect those with sensitivities. "Sugar-Free" often translates to the absence of conventional sugar, yet these products may be laden with alternative sweeteners that carry their own health implications, such as artificial sweeteners like Aspartame, Sucralose, or Stevia. These alternatives, while not contributing to sugar intake in the traditional (or most thought of) sense, are not free from controversy regarding their long-term health effects. Studies have shown varying outcomes on the metabolic and psychological effects of artificial sweeteners, including potential links to increased sugar cravings and disrupted gut microbiota.

The labeling of products as "Fat-Free" is a marketing strategy that, on the surface, appeals to health-conscious consumers looking to reduce their fat intake. However, this term carries with it a multitude of hidden implications that are not immediately apparent to the average shopper. While it suggests a healthier alternative by highlighting the absence of fat, what it often fails to disclose is the process manufacturers undertake to replace the flavor and texture typically provided by natural fats. This process frequently involves the addition of sugar, artificial flavors, or various thickening agents designed to mimic the mouthfeel and satisfaction that fat provides. The consequence of removing natural fats from food products is not merely a matter of subtracting calories or harmful dietary elements; it is also about what is added in place of those fats.

The addition of sugars, whether in the form of high fructose corn syrup, concentrated fruit juice, or other sweeteners, can significantly increase the caloric content of the food. Moreover, these sugars do not offer the same satiety that fats do, potentially leading to increased consumption as the body seeks to satisfy its energy needs. The artificial flavors and thickeners, while effective in enhancing taste and texture, contribute little to no nutritional value, and in some cases, may even pose health risks if consumed in large quantities over time. This practice of substituting fats with less nutritious or more calorie-dense ingredients raises questions about the true healthfulness of "Fat-Free" products. While they may offer a reduction in dietary fat, this is often at the expense of an overall nutritional balance. The higher the sugar content, the higher that it can contribute to a host of health issues, including weight gain, insulin resistance, and an increased risk of diabetes and heart disease. . . . Furthermore, the absence of natural fats eliminates a key source of essential fatty acids and fat-soluble vitamins, which are crucial for various bodily functions, including hormone production, cell structure maintenance, and nutrient absorption. . . .

The landscape of food labeling is a minefield of semantics, where terms are legally defined within margins that sometimes only technically align with consumer expectations. The FDA is especially malicious, in my personal opinion, because it allows the use of dangerous chemicals in agriculture, food additives, and food processing techniques. For example, allegations from critics of food safety practices have taken the FDA to task for permitting the use of carbon monoxide gas mixtures by meat producers in packaging, a method employed to maintain the meat's red color and potentially mask indications of spoilage from buyers.[1] The FDA was also challenged for allegedly allowing dairy cows to be treated with a special hormone, called recombinant bovine growth hormone (rBGH). This hormone makes the cows produce more of a substance in their milk called insulin-like growth factor 1 (IGF-1), which is higher than in milk from cows not given the hormone. Some people worry that IGF-1 could help tumors grow (though there is little proof that IGF-1 from milk affects tumor growth in humans). The FDA said it was okay to use this hormone in 1993, believing that the amount of IGF-1 humans get from drinking this milk wouldn't really affect them.[2] And it's worth noting that since 1993, all European Union (EU) countries have maintained a ban on rBGH use in dairy cattle.

It gets better, though: In 1994, the FDA found itself at the center of controversy and criticism for its policies regarding the routine administration of antibiotics to healthy livestock.[3] This practice, primarily aimed at promoting faster growth and increasing the efficiency of meat production, had come under intense scrutiny. Critics argued that such widespread, non-therapeutic use of antibiotics in animals that are not sick is a significant contributing factor to a pressing and global public health concern: the emergence and proliferation of antibiotic-resistant bacteria. Antibiotic resistance represents one of the most daunting challenges in modern medicine, rendering previously manageable infections increasingly difficult—and sometimes impossible—to treat. The crux of the issue lies in the biological arms race between bacteria and the drugs designed to kill them. Every time an antibiotic is used, it applies evolutionary pressure on bacteria, leading to the survival and proliferation of strains that can withstand the drug's effects. When antibiotics are used extensively in livestock, the likelihood of developing resistant bacteria in these animals increases. These bacteria can then be transmitted to humans through various pathways, including direct contact with animals, consumption of undercooked or improperly handled meat, and environmental contamination.

The process of cloning animals and using their meat for consumption is also being sanctioned by the FDA.[4] Its decision to authorize the sale of food products made from cloned animals is a move that has sparked controversy due to the lack of requirement for special labeling to distinguish these products from those obtained through traditional farming methods. Despite the groundbreaking nature of this decision, there is a consensus among experts that products originating from cloned animals may not be available on the U.S. market for several years due to various factors, including public skepticism and the technical challenges associated with cloning processes. Furthermore, it has been highlighted that regulatory bodies currently do not possess the legal mandate to enforce the labeling of products derived from cloned animals, leading to concerns about consumer rights and the transparency of food sources. This situation underscores a broader debate regarding the ethical implications of biotechnological advancements in food production and the adequacy of existing regulatory frameworks to address the complexities introduced by such innovations.

My personal stance leans strongly against the involvement of government in our lives, particularly when it comes to the oversight of our food's safety. The notion of a governmental body overseeing this, especially given the widespread corruption that plagues many such entities (not only the FDA), fills me with discomfort. The reliability of food labeling, the accuracy of portion sizes provided by the private sector, and the truthful representation of a product's potential harm all come into question. How can we discern what's truly beneficial or detrimental to our health amidst these uncertainties? These concerns are valid and provoke deep unease about whether government or even the private sector has our best interests at heart in these matters. . . . In an ideal world, the most reliable way to ensure the quality and safety of our food would be to cultivate it ourselves. This approach guarantees knowledge of its origin and the health benefits it provides. However, the demands of modern life, including the necessity of full-time employment for most, make this solution seem unattainable. This presents a significant challenge, forcing us to navigate the complexities of ensuring the quality of our food within the constraints of our busy lives.

Parallel to the evolution of food consumption is the rise in prescription drug use among Millennials. A generation labeled as the most anxious yet,[5] the rapid increase of—and overall push towards—medications for both physical and mental health issues is telling of the times. The reasons are manifold: From the pressures of a rapidly changing world to the destigmatization of mental healthcare. However, this uptick in pharmaceutical reliance raises questions about the long-term effects on public health and society's approach to wellness and illness.

The only method in the modern world of treatment appears to be primarily through medications. Research has shown that the increased reliance on medication is not solely a reflection of higher incidence rates of diseases but also a consequence of a broader shift in societal attitudes towards health and wellness.[6] This shift is partly due to greater awareness and diagnosis of health issues that were previously undiagnosed or stigmatized, coupled with a healthcare system that often prioritizes quick, pharmacological solutions over more time-consuming, non-pharmacological interventions.

The normalization of prescription medication as a primary form of treatment has indeed provided many individuals with much-needed relief and improvement in quality of life. Medications for conditions such as anxiety, depression, and ADHD, which are notably prevalent among Millennials, have become more accessible and socially acceptable to use. However, this trend also sparks a critical examination of our healthcare systems and societal norms, questioning whether our current approach might be too narrow, potentially overlooking holistic and preventative measures that could be equally or more effective for certain individuals and conditions.

Moreover, the long-term implications of widespread prescription drug use on public health are complex and multifaceted. On one hand, there are concerns about the potential for dependency, side effects, and the impact of long-term medication use on physical and mental health. On the other, there is the positive aspect of reducing immediate suffering and enabling individuals to function in their daily lives. This dichotomy highlights the need for a balanced approach that not only addresses symptoms but also focuses on underlying causes, lifestyle factors, and preventive care.

The conversation about the rise in prescription drug use among Millennials is also opening up discussions on alternative and complementary approaches to healthcare. There is a growing interest in lifestyle interventions, mindfulness, therapy, and natural remedies as complements or alternatives to pharmacological treatment. This broadening of the healthcare perspective acknowledges the multifactorial nature of health and wellness, suggesting that a more integrative approach could benefit individuals and society as a whole.

As we continue to navigate the complexities of modern healthcare and societal well-being, it is crucial to foster an environment where individuals feel supported in exploring a range of treatment options. This includes increasing access to mental health services, encouraging open dialogues about health and wellness, and promoting research into comprehensive care strategies. Ultimately, the goal is to create a more nuanced and adaptable healthcare system that responds to the needs of a diverse population, offering a spectrum of options to support both physical and mental health in a way that respects individual preferences and circumstances.

Air quality issues have intensified notably in our urban landscapes, paralleling the rise of technological advancements and widespread urbanization. This trend poses a significant threat to those who have grown up amidst these rapid changes. As cities swell, they accumulate higher levels of harmful pollutants—particulate matter, nitrogen dioxide, and sulfur dioxide being primary culprits. These pollutants, primarily from vehicle emissions, industrial activities, and the burning of fossil fuels, mar the very air we breathe.

The ramifications for Millennials are profound. Poor air quality not only degrades physical health, manifesting as respiratory and cardiovascular diseases but also subtly undermines cognitive functions, affecting concentration and productivity. Urban areas, despite being hubs of innovation and opportunity, thus also double as centers of heightened pollution exposure. The situation is ironical yet critical, demanding an urgent reevaluation of environmental policies and personal lifestyle choices to safeguard health and wellbeing in these burgeoning cityscapes. . . . Millennials, drawn to cities for work and lifestyle opportunities, find themselves at the frontline (and often taking the burden) of this environmental battle. Studies have shown that long-term exposure to poor air quality can lead to a myriad of health issues, from respiratory problems like asthma and bronchitis to cardiovascular diseases.[7]

Beyond the physical health implications, recent research has begun to shed light on the cognitive impact of air pollution. Exposure to high levels of air pollutants has been linked to decreased cognitive performance, increased risk of neurodegenerative diseases, and even changes in behavior.[8],[9],[10] This rapidly growing field of study suggests that the air quality crisis may also be a crisis of cognitive wellbeing, with Millennials potentially bearing the brunt of these effects as they age. The impact of air pollution is not felt equally across society, though. Lower-income families and those living in densely populated urban areas often bear a disproportionate burden.[11] These neighborhoods, frequently situated near industrial sites or congested highways, are exposed to higher levels of harmful pollutants. This disparity in air quality exacerbates existing health inequities, putting vulnerable populations at greater risk of both the physical and cognitive effects of pollution.

Innovations in technology offer promising solutions for mitigating air pollution. The transition to renewable energy sources, such as wind and solar, reduces dependence on fossil fuels, a major source of urban air pollution. Electric vehicles (EVs) and advancements in public transportation infrastructure can significantly cut down on vehicular emissions, one of the primary contributors to urban air quality issues. But these purported innovations are accompanied by a myriad of negative consequences, such as the environmental impact of producing and disposing of EV batteries, the intermittent nature of renewable energy sources requiring reliable storage solutions, and the significant financial investments needed for infrastructure development. Moreover, the production and recycling processes for solar panels and wind turbines pose environmental challenges, including the use of rare earth metals and the creation of hazardous waste. The production of electric vehicle batteries involves mining for lithium, cobalt, and nickel, processes that can lead to environmental degradation and raise ethical concerns regarding labor practices in mining communities. Additionally, the end-of-life disposal of these batteries poses significant environmental hazards if not properly managed, including the potential for soil and water contamination.

Renewable energy sources like wind and solar power are pivotal in the transition away from fossil fuels. However, their variability and reliance on weather conditions necessitate advancements in energy storage technologies to ensure a stable and reliable power supply. This challenge underscores the need for continuous innovation in battery technology and alternative storage solutions, such as pumped hydro storage or compressed air energy storage, which themselves carry environmental footprints that must be carefully managed.

The implementation of these technologies often requires substantial upfront investment, both from public and private sectors. This financial barrier can slow down the adoption of green technologies in lower-income regions or countries without the fiscal capacity to invest in such infrastructure. The economic challenge extends to consumers, many of whom may find the cost of transitioning to EVs or installing solar panels prohibitively expensive without governmental subsidies or incentives. Clearly, the technology isn't there yet to help the situation in a clean and cost-effective way for everyone. . . .

But there is hope. To effectively tackle the air quality crisis, a holistic approach that considers the environmental, economic, and social dimensions of these solutions is essential. This includes developing comprehensive recycling programs for batteries and solar panels to mitigate the environmental impact of their disposal and investing in research to find more sustainable materials and production methods. It also entails creating financial models and policies that make green technologies accessible to a broader segment of the population, ensuring that the benefits of cleaner air are equitably distributed. After all, we all need clean air to survive and thrive on this planet.

Public education and engagement are crucial in this endeavor, as widespread support and understanding of the importance of clean air and the role of technology in achieving it are necessary for meaningful change. Governments, industries, and communities must work together to foster innovation that is both environmentally sustainable and socially responsible.

Millennials (and frankly everyone on Earth) are clearly dealing with lots of big issues like pollution, climate change, food safety, and health problems from medicines and drugs; but Millennial's comfort with technology, passion for making a difference for the planet, and growing influence in society give them a strong voice. They are pushing for smarter, eco-friendly ideas: using green technology, demanding corporate and governmental accountability, and advocating for policies that support sustainable innovation. This way, they are helping shape a future where everyone has the chance to live happy and healthy lives.

Reader's Group Discussion Questions

- Considering the shift from locally sourced, unpro-
  cessed foods to today's global, processed diet,
  how do you think this evolution has directly impacted Millennials' physical and mental health?
  Discuss the role of nostalgia versus actual quality
  degradation in perceptions of food over generations.

- Given the complexities and potential misleading
  nature of food labels (e.g., "Gluten-Free," "Sugar-
  Free," "Fat-Free"), what measures can consumers
  take to better understand what they're eating?
  Discuss the responsibilities of corporations and
  regulatory bodies like the FDA in ensuring food
  safety and honesty in labeling.

- Reflect on the factors contributing to the increased reliance on medications among Millennials. How do societal changes and the destigmatization of mental healthcare play into this trend?
  Discuss the long-term implications of this reliance
  for individual health and public healthcare systems.

- Explore the connection between air quality and
  cognitive health, particularly in urban environments where Millennials are concentrated. How
  does this issue intersect with social and economic
  disparities, and what solutions could be proposed
  to address these challenges equitably?

- Discuss the potential and challenges of green technologies and renewable energy sources in mitigating environmental issues like air pollution. Consider the environmental, economic, and social factors that influence the adoption and effectiveness of these technologies.

- Given Millennials' unique position as digital natives, social activists, and emerging leaders, how can they leverage these roles to address the challenges outlined in the chapter? Discuss specific actions Millennials can take to promote sustainable innovation, demand accountability, and foster a healthier, more equitable future.

- How much of the responsibility for addressing issues like poor diet, reliance on medications, environmental pollution, and climate change should fall on individuals, and how much should be on systemic, societal changes? Discuss examples of how individual actions can lead to broader societal impacts and consider where the balance might lie between personal choices and the need for collective action.

Footnotes:

[1] Schaarsmith, Amy Mcconnell. February 19th, 2006. Pittsburgh Post Gazette. "Some raising red flag over use of gas to keep meat in the pink". https://www.-post-gazette.com/life/food/2006/02/19/Some-raising-red-flag-over-use-of-gas-to-keep-meat-in-the-pink/stories/200602190265

[2] Juskevich, J., & Guyer, C. (1990). Bovine growth hormone: human food safety evaluation. https://doi.org/10.1126/science.2203142

[3] Myllys V, Honkanen-Buzalski T, Huovinen P, Sandholm M, Nurmi E. Association af changes in the bacterial ecology of bovine mastitis with changes in the use of milking machines and antibacterial drugs. Acta Vet Scand. 1994;35(4):363-9. doi: 10.1186/BF03548309. PMID: 7676918; PMCID: PMC8101387.

[4] Catherine Larkin, "Cloned Animals Are Safe for U.S. Food, Agency Says (Update7)", found ay Bloomberg.com website. Accessed January 15, 2008. https://www.bloomberg.com/news/articles/2008-01-15/cloned-animals-may-be-used-for-food-in-u-s-fda-says

[5] Scott, Jody. January 8th, 2018. Vogue. "Why millennials are the most anxious generation in history". https://www.vogue.com.au/beauty/wellbeing/why-millennials-are-the-most-anxious-generation-in-history/news-story/755e7b197b-db20c42b1c11d7f48525cd#:~:text=So%20it's%20no%20surprise%20recent,the%20future%20or%20uncertain%20situations.

[6] Hagstrom, B., Mattsson, B., Wimo, A., & Gunnarsson, R. (2006). More illness and less disease? A 20-year perspective on chronic disease and medication. Scandinavian Journal of Public Health, 34, 584 - 588. https://doi.org/10.1080/14034940600703407.

[7] Lee, B., Kim, B., & Lee, K. (2014). Air Pollution Exposure and Cardiovascular Disease. Toxicological Research, 30, 71 - 75. https://doi.org/10.5487/TR.2014.30.2.071.

[8] Nephew, B., Németh, A., Hudda, N., Beamer, G., Mann, P., Petitto, J., Cali, R., Febo, M., Kulkarni, P., Poirier, G., King, J., Durant, J., & Brugge, D. (2020). Traffic-related particulate matter affects behavior, inflammation, and neural integrity in a developmental rodent model.. Environmental research, 183, 109242 . https://doi.org/10.1016/j.envres.2020.109242.

[9] Kilian, J., & Kitazawa, M. (2018). The emerging risk of exposure to air pollution on cognitive decline and Alzheimer's disease – Evidence from epidemiological and animal studies. Biomedical Journal, 41, 141 - 162. https://doi.org/10.1016/j.bj.2018.06.001.

[10] Ren, T., Yu, X., & Yang, W. (2019). Do cognitive and non-cognitive abilities mediate the relationship between air pollution exposure and mental health?. PLoS ONE, 14. https://doi.org/10.1371/journal.pone.0223353.

[11] Jbaily A, Zhou X, Liu J, Lee TH, Kamareddine L, Verguet S, Dominici F. Air pollution exposure disparities across US population and income groups. Nature. 2022 Jan;601(7892):228-233. doi: 10.1038/s41586-021-04190-y. Epub 2022 Jan 12. PMID: 35022594; PMCID: PMC10516300.

[what we think about when we think about blue-collar work]

Blue-collar work, unlike its white-collar counterpart, often carries an undeserved stigma of "lowly status"—a term I use broadly to capture its varied implications. From personal experience, this perception seems particularly pronounced among those shielded by a thin layer of privilege. While working in their lavish homes as a plumber and gas contractor, I often felt reduced to a mere footnote in their lives, perceived merely as someone there to maintain their luxurious lifestyles. The grandeur of mansions and estates did little to shield me from feeling like an inconvenience, a mere obstacle in their daily routine. This sentiment, though personal, is not unique to me; I've found it resonantly shared among my fellow tradespeople, and it deeply saddened me to no end. . . .

I do not know why there was (or is) this possible stigma attached to blue-collar work. Admittedly, I, too, had thought of it as something to be ashamed of. It may be because it invokes sentiments of a person undergoing harsh and taxing struggles of getting by that most would feel is unnecessary in regards to making a buck. I never really knew why I personally felt that way. I just knew, looking back now, that I had always viewed that kind of hands-on work as having the darkest of futures: constant physical pain, years shaved off your life both literally through your outward appearance and through the sheer toll it takes on your mind, body, and spirit.

Generally speaking, the reality of the matter is that nearly all of our occupations, in one way or another, cause us some kind of general disdain and an apparent, taxing, emotional loss in life. It does take sacrifice to gain stability, routine, and comfortability—the hallmarks that, whether we like it or not, are the backdrops of what we all view as "The American Dream," whatever we collectively view that may be at this point. The real hope is that the rat race will finally pay off in the end. But blue-collar work . . . why is it so different in the eyes of those who do not favor them and their value? Could it be because it's so tough to do, so tough to learn, and so tough to grasp? It is because of the discomfort, or possibly how dirty and gross it is? I've tried to unpack this many times.

When I first set my sights on a career in construction, I didn't realize just how much I lacked in mechanical skills. A lot of this was because I didn't have a father around during my early years to teach me how things worked—how to take them apart, understand them, and put them back together. Alternatively, it might have been simply a lack of interest on my part. . . . Reflecting on my teenage years, things changed when my mother remarried. My stepfather came into my life full of enthusiasm to pass on these mechanical skills. Despite his eagerness, I resisted. Perhaps it was my stubborn streak, or maybe I didn't warm up to him as my new father figure, or it could have been just typical teenage rebellion. I was more interested in making YouTube videos and hanging out with friends than in learning practical skills.

I quickly learned through being at the bottom of the totem pole of construction sites that the true reasoning for the disdain for blue-collar work is mostly because (1) The culture itself breeds a rugged, filthy person, and (2) Any prospective individual who shows enthusiastic interest in such occupations could easily be pushed away and dissuaded from continuing the journey, purely due to others on the job-site doing it for so long and becoming jaded in themselves and the trade. The culture, quite literally, wants you to quit.

The work is not only physically demanding but mentally and emotionally demanding, too. Those with higher knowledge of the trade than you make it abundantly clear that they are the true king of their dojo. That you are on *their* job-site. In their eyes, you are a liability, you are scum, and you aren't to be listened to, talk to, or heard. The only thing you are to do is nod your head at the orders they give, and at the end of the week, when your small check comes in for the torturous and grueling work you just did, you have to smile and pretend that the money you are receiving is five or ten times bigger than what the reality is. . . . It is a complete and total breakdown of the soul and of the human spirit. And this is why most men and women do not make it in blue-collar work.

Most trade school programs often offer a tempting promise: become a master or a top-tier professional in just a few years—maybe three, four, or five. But the reality of reaching your full potential in a trade can stretch much longer, often between one to two decades. This extended timeline might sound exaggerated to some, especially those who know someone who quickly climbed to the top of their field. Indeed, there are exceptional individuals who excel rapidly within their trades, mastering skills and earning well in a short time. But these high achievers are the exception rather than the rule. Despite this, many tradespeople might boast as if they are among the rare few who excelled quickly. This could be due to pride, ego, or simply the desire to stand out among peers who share similar goals. For those who are not prodigies, the journey can seem daunting. Often, they may project confidence and success, perhaps more than what is accurate, possibly to maintain their standing or inspire confidence in their abilities. The truth is that mastering a trade to the point of comfortable living takes time, dedication, and often, more than just a few years.

It is no secret that the trades are rife with rugged, tough men seemingly carved out of hypothetical wood. In fact, I would wager that the very essence of blue-collar work is predicated on how "badass" and tough you are. It is seen as complementary and worthy of bragging rights within construction work to be doing the worst, harshest, or most grueling part of the job, coupled with long hours, low pay, and even injuries to boot. Perhaps it showcases your vigor, determination, and drive towards the trade at hand. Perhaps your very work ethic defines you as a man, as if what makes you a "man" is defined by how much inconveniences you can handle and survive past. For every tough life choice you make it past, so it would seem, that "tough life choice" is just another notch in your belt of *manhood*.

This very mindset has bothered me for the majority of my adulthood because its toxicity almost percolates into every facet of the adult world. It is seen as virtuous in business to have survived hardships, big and small. It is seen through the selfish, capitalistic lens of a prospective boss's eye: this person, this worker bee I'm looking to hire, cannot only accept the harshest of life's tribulations and work-related messes, but they can seemingly will and hurdle themselves forward into the abyss of fantastical greener grass. In the eyes of a boss or owner of a company, this is seemingly seen as some of the most virtuous of all prospective new hires. But I digress. . . .

Ambition is the lifeblood of "The American Dream." Ambition is the sole reason for waking up for work in the morning. We are led to believe that ambition is what motivates and drives us towards success—and to some extent, it does drive all of us when we find that dare-to-be-great situation (or occupation) that makes us feel genuine giddiness for what is in store for our future. But for most people, ambition seems to be secondary to what is really driving the lifeblood of America: the fear of *individual social downfall*.

I've come up with the term "Individual Social Downfall" to describe the loss of one's material and philosophical standing in American society. This term captures the fear and potential reality of losing your home, failing to provide for your family, or letting down your loved ones. It highlights the darker side of ambition—the unintended consequences that can follow when we strive to climb higher. As the old saying goes, "What goes up, must come down." This concept reminds us that the pursuit of success often comes with risks.

For every single endeavor that there is to pursue, there will always be a sacrifice. And working with your hands or in mechanical work is no exception. The reality of it is that nobody can B.S. something that requires you to fix it because you would have to know how it functions and how it runs in order to get it to work properly. If it doesn't work, you therefore fail in the pursuit. If it doesn't showcase results, it is a failure. It seems as though the biggest flaw that Millennials have to deal with is the flaw of instant success.

To put it simply, it seems that Millennials have a greater aversion to failure than they have an appreciation for the rewards of success. In blue-collar work, success often comes from constant trial and error—persevering through failures until you finally fix something on your own. There's a deep satisfaction in taking something broken and restoring it to working order. Millennials appear to struggle with this process. Many Millennial students are showing less interest in traditional subjects like classical math and mechanics. They are also less inclined towards group-based learning methods and show a preference for digital over non-digital media.[1] They often lack the patience needed for the repetitive and sometimes frustrating nature of trial-and-error that defines much of blue-collar work.

Simon Sinek, viral social media influencer and self-help guru, put it simply when talking about what it takes to build meaningful relationships in this life: "There is no app for that, they are slow, meandering, uncomfortable, messy processes."[2] It, too, seems to reflect how or what Millennials lack when we talk about building a skill, career, or goal as adults. This instant drawing of dopamine from messages, apps, social media, viral ten-second videos, and mindless scrolling to infinity has poisoned our collective minds into a state of needing to obtain fixes inside a frantic, fast-paced competitive environment that doesn't physically exist. It's all virtual, but it all seems to engulf our brains more than our real life. Technology has become an extension of ourselves.

I suppose this entire chapter/essay is an axiom of something much larger than blue-collar work specifically. I suppose what I'm articulating can be applied to all levels of occupations and trades. Through time, dedication, discipline, grit, and a little bit of luck (or a lot a bit of luck), you, too, can succeed within your chosen field. This is what is universally told to us. It's the heart of what it means to live in America.

I will say this about blue-collar work—or any skilled work for that matter: You should always go into it with the mindset of simply learning something new for the sake of shelving it for future's sake. To give an example, as you work in trades you start to realize that all levels of mechanical work do have a set of rules that nearly all of them have to follow. Nuts and bolts sometimes need washers for certain metal applications. Rubber can't withstand this or that pressure. Learning to read labels on car parts, or any manufacturer part for anything mechanical. Once you start learning how metals and applications of fastening or sealing (or sealants) or even how liquids or cleaners function, you start to notice something: Almost all facets of everyday life apply to this knowledge. The world around us does in fact follow rules and guidelines nearly in every way, regardless of where you are in the world. Sure, you could have slight changes, like differences in our Imperial System versus the Metric System, but overall the knowledge can be applied and used just the same.

The knowledge you gain, my fellow Millennials, can be used to help you save money or pull you out of a bad spot in life. Things like changing a tire come to mind—which you'd be shocked to discover just how many people don't know how to do.[3] How a household cleaner reacts to specific metals, woods, or plastics. How and why things leak. Why things have to be maintained. How to maintain said things. Being able to help others, loved ones, or family out of a bind. Moving things forward. Even buying yourself time in order to get to a professional in whatever thing you need fixing or doing. I think some Millennials, young people, teenagers, and even those sheltered, older, or inexperienced lose this wealth of knowledge that can be beneficial, saving money and time for your life. Give you less panic and stress, simply by the confidence in yourself that you know you will be ready to take on any curveball life throws your way. This confidence is empowering. And my personal theory is that this epidemic of anxiety and depression rampant in our internet youth further contributes to these mental health ailment's crippling hold on us, making our lives feel worse. Panic and desperation can, too, make one more susceptible to being scammed or taken advantage of. This is something I think gets lost in translation when thinking of what it means to learn valuable tools to better prepare you for adulthood.

The term "adulting" often comes up when discussing Millennials and their approach to adulthood. This includes their efforts to establish independence, understand societal structures, and navigate the complexities of life. Mastering these aspects is crucial for their future success. As Millennials confront the harsh realities of life, their experiences shape their worldview, influencing their spending habits and voting behaviors. It's easy to see how this might frustrate older generations, like the Baby Boomers, who often feel they gained confidence in adulthood through practical experience and street smarts. These generational differences in handling life's challenges can lead to differing perspectives on what it means to be an adult. And the polls and surveys of Millennials via the *Associate Press*[4] back this claim of not knowing the proper navigation of life:

Fifty-seven percent of Gen-Zers and Millenials [*sic*] say they do not feel like they have adulting figured out. In the survey, 63% of Gen-Zers and Millennials said they did not feel like they were prepared for the responsibility of being an adult, and admitted they feel burned out by adulthood.¶ The biggest struggle for both generations seems to revolve around cars with 63% of the younger generations having no idea how to change the oil in a car, 48% not knowing how to change a tire and 42% not knowing how to jumpstart a car.

It is a disappointing reality that deserves attention. Consider all the basic tasks that financially struggling Millennials and Gen-Zers could have learned to do themselves, potentially saving hundreds, if not thousands, of dollars in mechanic fees. I'd imagine that these fees often seem to provide mechanics with a good laugh on their way to the bank. But it's not always the fault of younger generations that they lack this knowledge. Sometimes, the responsibility lies with their elders for not passing down these practical skills. The discussion continues in the same article, which claims:

Moreover, one in three Gen-Zers and Millenials [*sic*] say they do not feel financially independent. As a result, parents are helping these younger generations stay "financially afloat."¶ More than 22% say their parents have helped with rent or mortgage in the past year, and 34% admit their parents gave them money (not as a gift) to help them pay for something within the last year.¶ "In fact, 41% feel like they rely too much on their family as an adult," the survey stated.¶ Almost 50% of both generations say they think they will feel most like an adult when they buy a house, but 49% do not think they will ever be able to afford one.

There is a thin line between what is helping and what is not help-ing for "tough love's" sake. It's easy for an elder to not help a struggling

Millennial get by and claim that they need to figure it out on their own. And in some cases, they do figure it out. But in many cases, it does more harm than good to let them sink or swim. Because sometimes, all that happens is they just keep sinking and sinking and never get out of the water, so to speak.

If you take a Millennial or Gen-Zer who is far behind in life and is not prepared for what adulthood has in store for them—and you simply toss them into an ocean 5 miles out[5]—they may very well sink to the point of no return. What I mean by this is that it may leave them jobless, homeless, without money, with mental health issues, loss of self-confidence, hatred of the world, hatred of themselves, drained and fed-up already out of the gates of adulthood. This all at the very beginning of the rat race. The "sink or swim" mentality can only work if said swimmer is prepared for the worst. But if you have a swimmer repeatedly sinking over and over, this could very well destroy and implode themselves into a hopeless world not helpful to you or anyone (i.e., radicalization, zero self-esteem, zero self-confidence, dating life nonexistent, involuntary celibacy, rejection of values, atheism, nihilism, the list goes on…).

Blue-collar work and hands-on skills have transformative potential for Millennials, offering more than just a paycheck. In fact, they offer a reservoir of invaluable life knowledge. Through the lens of a tradesperson, one discovers that mechanical work adheres to its own set of universal principles. It's a world where nuts and bolts, washers and metals, mesh in orchestrated harmony. Understanding how materials interact and why certain tools and techniques are employed unveils a deeper truth: The rules governing the mechanical realm parallel the very essence of our everyday lives.

This wealth of practical knowledge isn't confined to workshops or garages. It extends its reach into the mundane tasks that shape our existence. Changing a tire, deciphering the labels on household products, discerning the nuances of leaks, or knowing when and how to maintain possessions—all of these skills serve as tools for navigating life's twists and turns. They bestow the power to lend a helping hand, not just to oneself, but to friends, family, or loved ones in need. The confidence born from this mastery is, in itself, a force that can weather the storms of life.

This lack of confidence is intrinsically linked to how Millennials perceive "adulting." It is a term that encapsulates the transition into independent living, the negotiation of societal norms, and the reckoning with life's harsh realities. For many Millennials, this journey can be a fraught one, marked by a sense of unpreparedness and a struggle to find one's footing. The statistics bear this out, with over half feeling ill-equipped for the responsibilities of adulthood. The challenges faced by Millennials in areas like automotive maintenance underscore the need for a reevaluation of how we equip our youth with practical life skills. The lack of basic automotive knowledge isn't just a minor inconvenience—it can have serious financial and emotional repercussions. It's a symptom of a larger issue: a generation struggling to find their place in a world they perceive as increasingly complex.

Furthermore, the financial struggles faced by many Millennials add an additional layer of complexity. It's a generation that, in significant numbers, doesn't feel financially independent. This reliance on family support, while sometimes necessary, can blur the lines between helpful assistance and a "sink or swim" mentality. In a world where housing prices soar and job markets fluctuate, the line between thriving and merely surviving becomes perilously thin.

We must bridge this gap between knowledge and practice, between theoretical adulthood and its gritty reality. Blue-collar work, with its hands-on ethos and practical applications, can be the very conduit that equips Millennials with the tools they need to navigate the maze of adulthood. It's not about simply staying afloat; it's about learning to sail through the storm.

Reader's Group Discussion Questions

- The chapter discusses the stigma attached to blue-collar work and the perception of individuals in these professions as having "lowly status." Why do you think society holds these stigmas against blue-collar workers, and what steps can be taken to change these perceptions?

- The author shares a deeply personal journey into the world of blue-collar work, including the initial lack of interest in mechanical skills and the eventual realization of their value. Have you ever experienced a change in perspective about a particular job or skill set? Share your story and what influenced this shift.

- The narrative highlights a disconnect between Millennials' upbringing, education, and tho practical skills required in blue-collar professions. How does the current educational system contribute to this gap, and what changes would you propose to better prepare young people for a diverse range of careers, including skilled trades?

- Discuss how the chapter portrays the psychological impact of blue-collar work on individuals, especially in terms of self-perception and societal valuation. How can communities and industries support the mental health and well-being of blue-collar workers?

- Considering the chapter's insights into the evolving nature of work, ambition, and the concept of "adulting," what do you think the future holds for the relationship between technology, education, and skilled labor? How can society ensure that essential skills are not lost to future generations while also embracing technological advancements?

Footnotes:

---

[1] Aktan, E., Pradhan, A., Sjoblom, K., Moon, F., Bartoli, I., Bayleyegn, Y., Cohen, B., & Kontsos, A. (2014). Challenges in Educating the Millennial Civil Engineers. , 1114-1125. https://doi.org/10.1061/9780784413357.100.

[2] Morning Future Staff. May 25th, 2020. *The Adecco Group*. "Simon Sinek's Advice: 'Millennials, Learn To Be Patient'". https://www.adeccogroup.com/future-of-work/latest-insights/simon-sineks-advice-millennials-learn-to-be-patient/
#:~:text=Millennials%20are%2C%20however%2C%20particularly%20prone,be%20cultivated%20and%20re%2Devaluated.

[3] Davies, Traverse. April 10th, 2019. *Medium*. "Changing a Tire is a Survival Skill". https://medium.com/dollarsurvival/changing-a-tire-is-a-survival-skill-fe167d72593a

[4] Yañez, Alejandra. March 18th, 2023. *KXAN*. "Over 50% of Gen Z, Millenials say they're not 'adulting' right: Report". https://www.kxan.com/top-stories/over-50-of-gen-z-millenials-say-theyre-not-adulting-right-report/amp/

[5] I'm saying this hypothetically and through the context of an individual's learning curve. Often most life events that are particularly difficult to pass through or understand are the equivalent to tossing someone in the ocean, as opposed to the deep end of a pool. In other words, the pool's deep-end is a relatively benign trail, while the ocean is something way more serious.

[the socialist millennial's disdain for American Capitalism: the good, the bad, and the ugly inside our hyper-meritocracy world]

Capitalism's hold on America is understandable. After all, it is true that Capitalism—as an economic system—has taken more people out of poverty than any other: In recent decades, significant economic growth has lifted many people out of poverty, reducing the global rate of extreme poverty to less than ten percent.[1] This progress is largely attributed to capitalist economic practices, which have been instrumental in facilitating this growth.

Whether it is true or not that Capitalism should take credit for lowering the world's poverty through time is elusive. It's easy to point to statistics and examples that prove or disprove the claim, just as it is for every opposing economic system like Socialism or Communism. Ask anyone with any confirmation bias, and you will quickly learn that they will give you just as many reasons why their ideas are superior to their opponent's. This is simply just human nature, and possibly the reason why we entertain ourselves with arguments/debate.

The love-child of Capitalism, and the queen of Objectivism, Ayn Rand, staunchly advocated for Laissez-Faire Capitalism in her works. She believed that this economic system is the most conducive to individual freedom, rational self-interest, and enriching prosperity. Rand argued that Capitalism, when implemented without government intervention, allows individuals to pursue their own goals and values, ultimately leading to a society that maximizes human potential.

One of Rand's fundamental assertions is that Capitalism aligns with human nature. She contended that individuals are inherently rational and should be free to pursue their own self-interest without coercion. In a Capitalist system, competition and voluntary exchange are key components, which Rand believed would lead to innovation, efficiency, and overall progress. Ayn Rand also argued that Capitalism provides the most just and ethical framework for a society. She believed that the principles of property rights and voluntary exchange are rooted in the respect for individual autonomy and consent. According to her, any form of forced wealth redistribution or government intervention infringes upon these rights and stifles personal liberty.

> "The moral justification of Capitalism is man's right to exist for his own sake, neither sacrificing himself to others nor sacrificing others to himself."   —Ayn Rand

Rand's perspective on Capitalism also emphasized the importance of *objective reality* and reason. She asserted that Capitalism relies on rational self-interest, where individuals make decisions based on a clear understanding of their own needs and desires. This, in turn (and in theory), leads to efficient resource allocation and the production of goods and services that genuinely benefit society.

Additionally, Rand highlighted the moral dimension of Capitalism. She argued that it is a system that rewards individual achievement and excellence, rather than promoting mediocrity or penalizing success. In her view, a capitalist society fosters a culture of ambition and aspiration, encouraging individuals to strive for their highest potential.

Rand believed that Capitalism leads to the greatest overall prosperity and standard of living. She pointed to historical examples where countries that embraced free-market Capitalism experienced rapid economic growth and improved living conditions for their citizens. She argued that competition and market forces drive efficiency, leading to a higher quality of life for all members of society.

It is important to note, however, that critics of Ayn Rand's views on Capitalism argue that her ideology may oversimplify the complexities of real-world economic systems.[2] They contend that unregulated Capitalism can lead to income inequality, exploitation, and the potential for market failures. They suggest that some level of government intervention may be necessary to address these concerns and ensure a fair and just society.

Ayn Rand's advocacy for Capitalism is grounded in her belief that it aligns with human nature, respects individual rights, and promotes rational self-interest. She argued that a laissez-faire capitalist system allows for maximum individual freedom and leads to a society that thrives on competition, innovation, and personal achievement. While her views are influential, it is important to consider the critiques and complexities surrounding the implementation of pure Capitalism in the real world. Balancing individual liberties with societal well-being remains a subject of ongoing debate in economics and philosophy.

The 2008 housing bubble and subsequent financial crisis marked a pivotal moment in the economic landscape of the United States.[3] For many Millennials, it was a formative experience that indelibly shaped their views on Capitalism and the economic system they inherited.

In the years leading up to the crisis, the housing market experienced an unprecedented boom. Dubbed the "housing bubble" by a man named Robert Shiller[4], this period saw a rapid escalation in property values, fueled by risky lending practices, speculative investment, and a general sense of economic euphoria. Financial institutions such as Morgan Stanley, Lehman Brothers, Goldman Sachs, JP Morgan Chase, and Bank of America, buoyed by a belief in the perpetual rise of housing prices, engaged in a complex web of mortgage-backed securities and derivatives.[5]

When the bubble burst, the repercussions were felt far and wide. Foreclosures skyrocketed, leading to a wave of evictions and a sharp decline in property values. Banks, heavily invested in mortgage-backed securities, faced insolvency. The crisis triggered a domino effect, sending shockwaves through the global financial system.

For Millennials, especially those coming of age during this tumultuous time, the effects were palpable. Many witnessed their parents grappling with the loss of homes, jobs, and savings. The traditional markers of financial security and stability that earlier generations took for granted suddenly seemed precarious.

The fallout from the 2008 crisis left an indelible mark on the collective psyche of Millennials. It eroded trust in financial institutions and raised questions about the efficacy and fairness of the capitalist system. The notion that hard work and responsible financial planning were guarantees of prosperity was shattered. Instead, they saw how systemic failures, greed, and reckless speculation could lead to widespread suffering. . . .

In the wake of the crisis, many Millennials began to view Capitalism through a more critical lens. They questioned the wisdom of an economic system that seemed to reward risky financial practices while leaving ordinary citizens to bear the brunt of the fallout. This skepticism extended beyond Wall Street, permeating discussions about income inequality, access to healthcare, and the affordability of education, chiefly through higher education.

As Millennials entered the workforce, they encountered an economy still recovering from the shockwaves of 2008. Job opportunities were scarcer, wage growth stagnated, and the burden of student loan debt became an albatross for many. This confluence of factors further fueled the sentiment that the system was fundamentally skewed against them.

In response to their disillusionment with Capitalism, as it had been practiced in the lead-up to the 2008 crisis, many Millennials began to advocate for reform. They sought a more inclusive and equitable economic system that prioritized the well-being of all citizens, not just the privileged few.

This movement towards a more socially conscious form of Capitalism, often associated with terms like "social democracy" or "democratic socialism," reflects a desire to temper the excesses of a hyper-meritocratic world. It calls for policies that address income inequality, provide robust social safety nets, and ensure access to affordable education and healthcare. . . . As I write this, it should be noted that these concepts and policies are not without flaws in logic, governmental corruption, and implementation challenges. The argument for a more socially conscious Capitalism acknowledges the imperfections and potential pitfalls inherent in any economic and social system, striving to address them proactively.

The 2008 housing bubble served as a wake-up call for Millennials, prompting them to critically examine the economic system they were inheriting. It ignited a collective introspection about the values and priorities that should underpin the capitalist framework. While their disdain for certain aspects of American Capitalism is rooted in this experience, it also fuels a passionate drive for a more just and inclusive economic order.

The dream of homeownership, once an emblem of the American Dream, now seems like an elusive mirage for many Millennials. The statistics paint a stark picture: a significant portion of this generation finds themselves unable to step onto the first rung of the property ladder.[6] This predicament has profound implications, not only for their economic prospects but also for their outlook on the very system that was supposed to enable their success.

The idea of owning a home, for the Millennial generation, can feel like a distant fantasy. Skyrocketing property prices, stagnant wages, and a mounting burden of student loan debt have converged to create a perfect storm. In major urban centers, the prospect of scraping together a down payment on a modest abode can seem like an insurmountable feat.[7] One of the main culprits driving this phenomenon is the steep rise in housing costs relative to income. In many metropolitan areas, housing prices have outpaced wage growth by a significant margin. The resulting gap between earnings and property values has left Millennials struggling to bridge the divide.

The burden of student loan debt further compounds the issue. Many Millennials are saddled with substantial educational loans, which can serve as a major deterrent to saving for a down payment. Instead of squirreling away funds for a future home, a significant portion of their income is allocated to servicing these debts. This debt dilemma not only inhibits the ability to save but also raises questions about the wisdom of entering into further financial commitments, such as a mortgage. The prospect of taking on additional debt can be a daunting one, particularly for a generation that witnessed the aftermath of the 2008 financial crisis.

In contrast to previous generations (i.e., baby boomers, etc.), Millennials are entering the housing market at a distinct disadvantage. The entry cost into the housing market has significantly increased, making it almost unaffordable for many. Additionally, there is a noticeable shortage of affordable housing, which further widens the homeownership gap between generations. This situation highlights the deep-rooted systemic issues that Millennials encounter, forcing them to reevaluate the realities of a capitalist system that no longer seems to provide a clear path to wealth and stability. For many, the dream of homeowner-ship—a key aspect of financial security—is becoming increasingly un-attainable, as it continues to drift out of reach.

For Millennials, this conundrum raises profound questions about the viability and fairness of the capitalist system. The belief that hard work and responsible financial planning would lead to prosperity has been eroded by the harsh realities of the housing market. Instead of reaping the rewards of their labor, many find themselves caught in a cycle of perpetual renting, with little hope of breaking free.

The inability to achieve homeownership has prompted many Mil-lennials to reevaluate their stance on Capitalism. The promise of up-ward mobility and financial security that underpins the capitalist ethos now seems like a distant promise. Instead, they are confronted with a system that appears to favor those who are already economically privi-leged. This disillusionment with Capitalism is not a rejection of the principles of hard work and personal responsibility. Rather, it is a recognition that the current iteration of the system may not be deliver-ing on its promises. The housing crisis has become a microcosm of the broader economic challenges faced by Millennials, and it has spurred a reexamination of the doctrines that underpin their worldview.

In many ways, the housing crisis encapsulates the economic strug-gles of the Millennial generation. The barriers to homeownership serve as a tangible reminder of the challenges they face. As they grapple with the realities of an increasingly unaffordable housing market, many Mil-lennials are questioning whether the current capitalist paradigm is tru-ly serving their best interests.

Ultimately, the housing crisis may very well be the catalyst that prompts Millennials to advocate for systemic change. It is a call to ac-tion, a demand for a more equitable economic system that provides genuine opportunities for prosperity and financial stability. The ques-tion that remains is whether society will heed this call and work to-wards a future where homeownership is not a distant dream, but an attainable reality for all. . . .

Let us discuss how baby boomers compare to Millennials in regards to housing and The American Dream. After all, it seems as though Boomers, the so-called parents of Millennials, have a mild disdain, disappointment, and annoyance for the Millennial mindset. The economic trajectories of Baby Boomers and Millennials unfold against vastly different backdrops. Baby Boomers entered a world characterized by unique opportunities and advantages, while Millennials find themselves contending with a markedly altered economic landscape. Several key factors contribute to this disparity.

Baby Boomers were born into an era of unparalleled economic growth following World War II. The post-war period saw a surge in industrialization, technological progress, and the opening of new industries. This led to a robust job market, rising wages, and a significant expansion of opportunities for employment and financial stability. One of the most significant advantages for Baby Boomers was the relative affordability of housing during their early adulthood. The housing market of the mid-20th century featured more moderate prices and fewer speculative investments. This allowed many Baby Boomers to enter the housing market at a relatively young age, providing them with a tangible asset and a source of wealth accumulation.

Millennials face a vastly different housing market. Skyrocketing property prices, stagnant wages, and a greater reliance on renting have made homeownership an elusive goal. This fundamental shift in the housing market has profound implications for Millennials' ability to build wealth and financial stability. Many Baby Boomers enjoyed long-term job security and robust benefits packages, providing them with a level of financial stability that has become increasingly rare for Millennials. Company loyalty and defined benefit pension plans were more common, offering a safety net for retirement planning.

On the other hand, Millennials have entered a job market characterized by greater volatility, a rise in contract and gig work, and a shift away from traditional pension plans towards defined contribution plans like 401(k)s. This shift has placed more responsibility on individuals to manage their retirement savings, often in the face of economic uncertainty. The cost of education has risen dramatically since the Baby Boomer generation. Many Baby Boomers were able to attend college with more manageable tuition fees and without the burden of significant student loan debt. This allowed them to enter the workforce without the financial albatross that many Millennials carry.

The rapid pace of technological advancement and globalization has transformed the economic landscape in ways that present both opportunities and challenges for Millennials. While these developments have created new industries and opportunities, they have also led to increased competition and a more fluid job market. For Baby Boomers, the economic landscape was far less globalized and technology-dependent. They often had more predictable career trajectories within stable industries. Millennials, on the other hand, must navigate an increasingly dynamic and interconnected global economy.

The economic disparities between Baby Boomers and Millennials arise from a complex interplay of historical, economic, and societal factors. While Baby Boomers enjoy a unique set of circumstances, Millennials must grapple with a markedly different economic landscape. Recognizing these differences is crucial for understanding the challenges Millennials face and for shaping policies and practices that promote economic equity and prosperity for all generations.

While Capitalism seems to be 100% positive, in theory, it is not the case in practice. The all-or-nothing, what's-mine-is-mine, dog-eat-dog society that fosters Capitalism does have a slew of issues that don't seem compatible with the human condition. While drive, ambition, hard work, and grotesque endurance are highly rewarded in that society, what is punished, it seems, are those who do not desire a grotesque lifestyle and want simple experiences and freedom. The conundrum that everyone in society faces is this: money equals freedom, but to gain money you have to work constantly in a way that makes you a slave to the very market that is supposedly enriching you. . . .

Most Americans—a whopping 63% of them—can't afford even something as simple as a 500$ car emergency.[8] It appears as though in Capitalism the margin of error is so razor thin to the point of being nonexistent. People can't afford emergencies, sick days, or even just a regular day off to mentally recoup and remain sane. This is because the bills and the income provided by most jobs within Capitalism are almost the same, even as you move up the ladder. The system does not account for saving or profit, unless you shackle yourself and repress needs and wants. This, in turn, renders you unfree. Capitalism creates the illusion and promise of freedom under the guise that "if you get the money, you will get the reward of freedom." But it does not tell you that those with more money have the power to keep those without money completely at bay and perpetually in the same tax bracket, year after year. Those with the money set the standard, and there isn't anything the government or the people can do about it.

It is true that sacrificing days off, morning coffee runs, eating out with friends and family, neglecting to buy things, and working constantly will eventually gain you surplus value, but unless you have a goal in mind to put said value into what will gain you value in the future, it almost always will be funneled back into everyday life. But the reality is that the competition within a capitalist society does not account for everyone to get a piece of the pie. By design, the system favors a select few, and sometimes it isn't even predicated on a good product or service. Sometimes, the key to success becomes how much money you dump into advertisement, media, or government play. The little bit of money itself that you work hard to get suddenly doesn't seem worth it to gamble on an endeavor filled with uncertainty.

Higher risk, higher reward, though they say. . . .

It would seem as though there isn't a healthy way out of the capitalistic system. Once in, it is nearly impossible to get out—and in more ways than one: mentally, it changes you; routine-wise, it drains you; your outlook, it gets poisoned, jaded, and hopeless. But this is only if you are sinking and not swimming. Obviously, those who are winning in the game of Capitalism feel very comfortable and enjoy their time on earth (and would probably want to keep the status quo). But for those that aren't, it seems to be a constant funk, a constant rat race where all you see is a machine that you are apart of that needs constant maintenance by any means necessary, including by way of your time, freedom, comfort, happiness, health, and overall well-being. Capitalism does not care if you sink. It does it no good if you are a sinker; it simply leaves you behind because you are deemed little in use.

But usefulness is completely subjective. If you do your job well and make money for the company, anyone who is above you can criticize your efforts and make you feel useless. If you do a job or task that makes money, the boss reserves the headache of telling you to work faster, harder, longer, and better than you are right then, because the goal is to nab more and more money. Bosses often use this card, too. Never mind the exhaustion. Never mind your mental state. You are a machine that is paid to do the company's bidding. And you are expected to care at (or more) than the company's owner's level, regardless if you are rewarded for it or not. "You should be happy to have the privilege of working here," is the mindset you are told, spoken or unspoken.

That's the epitome of hyper-capitalism; the money comes first before the human. And sometimes the mere value in your youth is what is demanded. For many young workers, particularly those with physical prowess, their value is often reduced to the strength of their back. It's a task assigned a monetary worth that rarely corresponds to the potential long-term physical toll. Once the body wears down, there's a line of fresh faces ready to step in. It's a stark reminder that, in this system, you serve a purpose until you no longer do, then you're replaced like a spent battery.

In the heart of Capitalism, the stark reality often unfolds: the harder you work, the less freedom you have to enjoy the fruits of your labor. It's a relentless cycle, where the pursuit of financial stability can ironically lead to a kind of bondage. In this all-or-nothing world, simplicity and the pursuit of genuine experiences sometimes seem like luxuries reserved for a select few. As you climb the ladder within this system, the financial calculus remains eerily constant. The promise of saving or profiting is elusive and often necessitates a life of self-restraint and deferred gratification. The illusion of freedom tied to financial success neglects to reveal the pervasive influence wielded by those who have already amassed wealth.

While sacrificing leisure and indulgence may eventually yield surplus value, the gamble is rarely guaranteed. The cutthroat nature of Capitalism often tips the scales in favor of a privileged few. Success can hinge not on the quality of a product or service but on the size of the advertising budget, media exposure, or political influence. For many, the prospect of risking hard-earned money on ventures fraught with uncertainty feels like a gamble not worth taking. Exiting the capitalist paradigm is akin to navigating a labyrinth with no clear exit. The toll it exacts is multifold: mentally, it reshapes your outlook; daily routines become draining rituals; and the once-rosy perspective on life becomes tinged with bitterness and resignation.

The fruits of one's labor, no matter how diligent or productive, can be dismissed or critiqued by those in positions of power. The ceaseless pursuit of profit places little value on individual well-being, and often the message is clear: you are but a cog in the machine, replaceable and expendable.

Reader's Group Discussion Questions

- What are your thoughts on Ayn Rand's philosophy that Capitalism is the most ethical and effective economic system for promoting individual freedom and prosperity? Do you see any flaws in her arguments?

- In what ways do you think the 2008 financial crisis has permanently altered Millennials' views on Capitalism and financial stability?

- How do the challenges Millennials face in the housing market reflect broader issues within the capitalist system? Do you believe these challenges are a result of systemic failures or individual circumstances?

- Reflect on the economic disparities between baby boomers and Millennials. To what extent do you think these differences are shaped by changes in the economy and society?

- Based on the chapter and your own experiences, has your view of Capitalism changed? Do you find yourself more sympathetic to the criticisms of Capitalism, or do you believe its benefits outweigh its drawbacks?

- Discuss amongst the group what exactly a world would look like under Laissez-Faire Capitalism. Tell the good, the bad, and the ugly.

Footnotes:

[1] Si, S., Ahlstrom, D., Wei, J., & Cullen, J. (2019). Business, Entrepreneurship and Innovation Toward Poverty Reduction. Entrepreneurship & Regional Development, 32, 1 - 20. https://doi.org/10.1080/08985626.2019.1640485.

[2] Cummins, Denise. February 16th, 2016. *PBS*. "Column: This is what happens when you take Ayn Rand seriously". https://www.pbs.org/newshour/economy/column-this-is-what-happens-when-you-take-ayn-rand-seriously

[3] Fox, Justin. November, 2013. *Harvard Business Review*. "What We've Learned from the Financial Crisis". https://hbr.org/2013/11/what-weve-learned-from-the-financial-crisis

[4] Lambert, Lance. July 24th, 2023. *Fortune*. "Robert Shiller—who called the 2008 housing bubble—thinks he knows how the housing market will exit its latest period of exuberance". https://fortune.com/2023/07/24/housing-market-robert-shiller-home-price-prediction-outlook/amp/

[5] Marquit, Miranda. August 26th, 2023. *Investopedia*. "Major Players in the 2008 Financial Crisis: Where Are They Now?". https://www.investopedia.com/insights/major-players-2008-financial-crisis-and-where-they-are-now/#:~:text=6 Some of the largest,government and did not fail.

[6] Myers, D., Lee, H., & Simmons, P. (2020). Cohort insights into recovery of Millennial homeownership after the Great Recession. Journal of Housing Economics, 47, 101619. https://doi.org/10.1016/J.JHE.2019.01.004.

[7] Carr, K., Herbert, C., Lam, K., & Makhkamov, Y. (2008). Rates of Foreclosure in Home and ADDI Programs. . https://doi.org/10.2139/ssrn.1582610.

[8] Konish, Lorie. August 31st, 2023. *CNBC*. "63% of workers unable to pay a $500 emergency expense, survey finds. How employers may help change that". https://www.cnbc.com/2023/08/31/63percent-of-workers-are-unable-to-pay-a-500-emergency-expense-survey.html

["the game of TikTok": popularity's hook on the internet generation's psyche]

Trying to understand the virality of internet videos is a fleeting conundrum. Back in the early days of MySpace, there wasn't a clear means of viewing videos on the internet. People would embed Quicktime videos and Windows Media Player plug-ins into their profiles. (These were the days when HTML coding was actually more hip, considering your profile on MySpace often told people who you were and how much effort you'd put into life.) Learning to design a page was an art form, and nearly everyone wanted to figure out how to put their favorite music video on their profiles. So much so that when you came across a friend that *did* have one, you most certainly were going to message them about it: "Where the HECK did you get that video?! How did you get that thing on your profile?!"

And then they would often (A) Tell you how they did it, or (B) Not tell you and basically gloat on their knowledge that someone they knew did not know how they did it. The "na-na-na-boo-boo" effect, I have coined. However, once YouTube finally caught on shortly thereafter, all you saw, and what you saw, was people posting embedded, shareable, high-quality videos on their profiles. It become an outlet for things to be easily accessible by an almost Google-like search bar.[1] People felt liberated in a way that had never been seen before. And make no mistake, a new Wild West was born—not the criminal type, to be sure, but the type of pro-Free Speech utopia that Americans longed for. The kind of speech so easily accessible and has far-reaching potential unforeseen or heard of in all of human history. In a sense, the virality gave the power of a platform to any and everyone who had something important to share.

But what was quickly realized is that "important" became subjective. Early cute cat videos went viral. Odd songs about "Chocolate Rain" became viral. Silly antics, big and small, were seen by millions for seemingly no rhyme or reason except for the fact that these videos were entertaining in a way that even now in modern times we still have no idea why. But rest assured, when you saw a viral video and what it looked like—even though you couldn't exactly pinpoint its entertainment value—you could look at the video's esthetics and say, "That is for sure a viral YouTube video."

Television and cable had a very particular way of advertising and gaining viewership. Concepts such as ratings, airtime, et cetera, were always seen as roadblocks to those who created content. The worldview of the average, up-and-coming YouTuber simply was that caring too much about views, ads, and airtime would taint and almost make the YouTuber in question a Holden Caulfield-like level of phony. Your authenticity was at stake when it came to your content. "Selling out" was a huge no-no. But then quickly something started to change.

YouTube more and more would push their already-established feature of subscriptions on their content creators. The idea was that if someone subscribed to you, (1) It would showcase hard numbers of dedicated users actively watching your content, (2) The user could prove they liked your content by their subscribing, and (3) Your content could be easier to view when it first would be published, driving up views . . . and so on. But this became reminiscent of the old days of television. And as YouTube went on—and subsequently Google bought the company—advertisement became the supreme feature of YouTube. It became the new television. Anyone could claim that this is the evolution of what we see television and viewing content as, and they would probably have a huge population of people who agree with them.

It quickly appeared that money always would follow the content. With seemingly unknown people going viral on YouTube, over and over again—creating their following of subscribers. It was easy for them to take on the role of *celebrity*, no matter how much Hollywood, the media, or anyone else tried to deny it. For the first time in media history, people were realizing that fame and fortune, quite literally, was completely predicated not on the status of where your content was being viewed, but by how many would view it and *continue* to view it. If you made a website or blog via a run-of-the-mill web-hosting website like GoDaddy, as long as people were watching what you were pushing—no matter what it was—you could gain fame and fortune. This shocked traditional viewers of media content who thought that talent and actual substance backed by a big production company was the sole way to build a career in media. No longer were the days where that was so. But with freedom, zero constraints from the media overlords, and complete liberation came the downside to a quickly over-saturated market of ideas: talentless individuals were the kings and queens of the space.

Though my usage of the word "talentless" is completely 100% grounded on whoever is the subjective viewer of such content creator, what remains is objective: The media was devolving rapidly along with our primitive and innate drive for entertainment. We craved stimulation, we craved dopamine. And these social media companies knew that. It seemed as though the top social media company of whatever timeframe would always be the one that drove the most traffic and kept the most users online and on their product for as long as humanly possible. Programmers were coming up with more efficient ways for users to consume the content most easily, rapidly, and in constant succession. While YouTube was still dominating the video space, it still took users some time to find and search for content they liked and could view for prolonged periods.

Vine was a short-form video hosting service that allowed users to create and share six-second looping video clips. Launched in 2013 by Dom Hofmann, Rus Yusupov, and Colin Kroll, Vine quickly gained popularity for its unique format and became a platform for creativity and entertainment. The app's success was partly due to its simplicity: Users could easily record and share brief, engaging videos. Vine's brevity encouraged creativity within constraints, leading to the rise of Vine celebrities who mastered the art of storytelling in just a few seconds. The platform became a hub for comedy sketches, music performances, and various other forms of content. And for a while, the short-form constraints fostered real content that had substance and true talent involved: coming up with an idea for a skit, executing it, and making it concise and relatable enough for viewers to keep watching. . . .

In 2012, Twitter acquired Vine before its official launch, integrating it into the social media landscape. The six-second time limit not only distinguished Vine from other video platforms but also contributed to its viral nature. The looping feature allowed users to watch short videos repeatedly, making it easy for content to go viral and gain widespread attention. Vine's community grew rapidly, with users experimenting with different genres and styles. Comedy emerged as a dominant category, with Vine stars like King Bach, Lele Pons, and Nash Grier amassing millions of followers. Brands and marketers also recognized the platform's potential for engaging a younger audience, leading to collaborations and sponsored content.

Despite its initial success, Vine faced challenges, including increased competition from platforms like Instagram and Snapchat, who quickly cloned and modified their sites to match the same hype and traffic that Vine was receiving. I guess those high on the ladder could not accept that their platform was old news and were clinging to the demands of users on a competition site to keep their companies afloat. Twitter, the owner of Vine and all its Intellectual Property (IP), was facing its own struggles, and this ultimately made it decide to discontinue Vine in 2016. The announcement was met with huge disappointment from users and content creators who had built their entire careers on the platform. The end of Vine, however, marked the beginning of a new chapter for many of its prominent creators. Many Vine stars transitioned to other platforms like YouTube and Instagram, leveraging their existing fan base to continue creating content. The closure of Vine highlighted the transient nature of social media platforms and the importance of adaptability for content creators.

In the years following Vine's closure, the short-form video format continued to thrive on other platforms. TikTok, launched in 2016, almost immediately after Vine's retirement, gained immense popularity by allowing users to create and share short videos set to music. TikTok's success demonstrated the enduring appeal of concise, entertaining content and the evolving preferences of online audiences. At least according to Forbes magazine.[2] But the quality of content was replaced by the virality of content. It was more profitable to get eyes on shock value, sex, or outrage than to produce insightful, helpful, entertaining, and talent-filled content. Trends on TikTok seem to showcase more and more people dancing in front of their cameras to snippets of the latest popular music. Then it wasn't enough. It had to be beautiful, conventionally sexy women in scantily clad outfits doing the dancing. It was saturated and shown repeatedly over and over, and people—probably mostly men—consistently ate it up. Over and over on YouTube around the Summer of 2018, all you would see was that repetitive dance video advertisement of floating TikTokers moving to the beat of Sub Urban's hit song "Cradles." And without the skip button. . . .

There became an almost hypnotizing effect to scrolling endlessly through the TikTok void. A mind-numbing trance that would take you down a virtually infinite amount of rabbit-holes. Time was being sucked away from you, swallowed up, and replaced by the burning sensation of completely wasting your waking moments. The same way a drug addict would feel, probably. I would wager that TikTok is just simply "digital drugs"; a way to cope with the stressors that life brings; a way to combat boredom and inject a constant stream of mindless entertainment into your psyche.

As a content creator, this is a perfect wet dream of attention, perceived validation, and pseudo-status that could only be quantified through the internet space. If you weren't constantly in the limelight and retaining your long-lasting "15 minutes of fame," as they say, you would be forgotten and replaced by another. And for a lot of creators, this felt like the ultimate rejection of your peers in this metaverse. Since everyone with an account is keenly aware of viral videos and what attention and perks they bring, there is no shortage of people churning out as much content as humanly possible, further solidifying and creating the infinity scroll of TikTok.

We are our own worst enemy, as they say.

What exactly would make someone even *want* to be viral? After all, wouldn't it be annoying to have constant people around you, deranged fans fawning over you, crawling on their hands and knees, clawing at you to sign something of theirs? I'm sure at first it would be interesting, but after the occurrence happening day after day, even when just going out to get something average like some daily groceries, I'm sure it would leave you feeling annoyed and like the fame itself is a sick curse. Once you are in the public eye and known for something that turns heads, it is easy to be recognized for your remaining days of that one singular thing. Your unknown existence that blended into the public landscape has vanished. All eyes are on you. Constant paparazzi, media heads, journalists, anyone and everyone trying to catch you slipping to put you in their next hit piece (or next nasty social media status for that, too, to go viral). You become a public commodity.

Society of the Spectacle, a non-fiction political theory and social philosophy masterpiece originally published in 1967 by Buchet-Chastel (French publishing house), explores the idea that modern society is dominated by images and representations, creating a spectacle that separates individuals from real, lived experiences. In the context of fame, Debord's concepts can be applied to understand how the media-driven spectacle influences the perception and construction of celebrity. Fame, in the *Society of the Spectacle*, becomes a spectacle itself. Celebrities are often portrayed and consumed as images, symbols, and narratives rather than as authentic individuals. The spectacle, according to Debord, is a social relationship mediated by images, where reality is replaced by representations. In the realm of fame, this means that the public often engages with celebrities through the lens of media representations, constructed narratives, and curated images.

> "The status of celebrity offers the promise of being showered with 'all good things' that Capitalism has to offer. The grotesque display of celebrity lives (and deaths) is the contemporary form of the cult of personality; those 'famous for being famous' hold out the spectacular promise of the complete erosion of an autonomously lived life in return for an apotheosis as an image. The ideological function of celebrity (and lottery systems) is clear—like a modern 'wheel of fortune' the message is 'all is luck; some are rich, some are poor, that is the way the world is...it could be you!"
>
> — Guy Debord, quote from *The Society of the Spectacle*

The celebrity, in this framework, becomes a commodity, a representation detached from the real person behind the fame. The public's perception is shaped not by direct experiences with the individual but by the images and stories presented through various media channels. This process reinforces the idea that the spectacle mediates our understanding of the world, including our perception of fame and those who achieve it. This conundrum of celebrity in and of itself may be perpetuating (and probably warping) our societal ideals of what success, grotesque accomplishments, and happiness really means. Debord argues that the spectacle serves to maintain the existing social order and reinforce consumerism. In the context of fame, this implies that celebrities often become symbols of success, aspiration, or certain societal ideals. Their images are commodified and consumed by the public as part of the larger spectacle, contributing to the perpetuation of certain values and norms. *Society of the Spectacle* provides a framework for understanding how fame operates within a media-saturated society. It highlights the role of images, representations, and narratives in shaping our perception of celebrities, emphasizing the detachment of fame from the lived experiences of individuals. The spectacle, according to Debord, influences not only how we perceive fame but also how it functions as a social and cultural phenomenon.

> **"The more he identifies with the dominant images of need, the less he understands his own life and his own desires. The spectacle's estrangement from the acting subject is expressed by the fact that the individual's gestures are no longer his own; they are the gestures of someone else who represents them to him."** — Guy Debord, quote from *The Society of the Spectacle*

The TikTok hook on both Gen-Z and Millennials seems to grabble their hearts and minds, planting the seed of hypothetical fame and fortune into an impressionable young person. It is reminiscent of a time when we all were in high school, looking up at those more beautiful, more popular, more smart, more kind, more funny, more insert <u>ANY-ADJECTIVE-THAT-YOU-ARE-NOT</u> here. Whatever it may be, we all seem to compare apples to oranges. No two humans are the same, but it is easy for us to forget that fact and constantly downplay ourselves to the point of depression and anxiety, tying back into the crux of Millennial mental turmoil.

Being popular and well-known is always something people will strive for, now and forever. The internet explodes and amplifies such popularity to the point of manufacturing comments and likes from faceless people who we assume are people (and not bots, scammers, or phishers). The internet is a tricky place to navigate. The dopamine fix that Millennials and Gen-Zers feel seems to stem from a yearning for likability. . . . But in a world of individuals who all have the same goal of popularity and likability, what gets lost in translation is that in order to receive likes, comments, and love, you have to, in turn, give more likes, comments, and love than you receive. The only true means of gaining a following or gaining traction in the social media landscape is to vehemently and constantly shell out positive and feel-good vibes. Unless of course your content is predicated on outrage and anger (i.e., the political landscape, mainstream media—like Fox News, CNN, MSNBC, etc.). Or the controversial pushing of ideas, techniques, situations, or feelings that people find uncomfortable to confront. . . .

It appears that this very prose you are reading falls under, admittedly, the latter category . . . or so I've been told.

Reader's Group Discussion Questions

- How has the shift from MySpace's HTML customization to TikTok's algorithm-driven content changed the way we perceive and engage with online content?

- In what ways has the pursuit of virality impacted the quality and substance of online content? Discuss examples of how "important" content is now defined.

- How do features like TikTok's endless scroll and algorithm preferences shape the creativity and authenticity of content creators?

- What are the psychological effects of pursuing virality and fame on social media? Consider the impact on content creators and their audiences.

- What are the broader societal implications of a platform like TikTok that prioritizes short, engaging content over depth and authenticity?

- How does Debord's theory apply to the modern spectacle of social media fame? Discuss the transformation of celebrities into commodities and the impact on individual authenticity.

- How has your own use of or engagement with social media platforms like TikTok influenced your perception of fame, popularity, and content value?

Footnotes:

[1] Oddly enough, Google acquired YouTube in the Fall of 2006 for a sum of 1.65 billion dollars. Since that day it seems to have never been the same YouTube it once was—a Wild West-like plethora of uncensored content (for the most part).

[2] Taulli, Tom. January 31st, 2020. *Forbes*. "TikTok: Why The Enormous Success?". https://www.forbes.com/sites/tomtaulli/2020/01/31/tiktok-why-the-enormous-success/amp/

CHAPTER SIX

["technology's corrosion of our collective minds": why we have poor attention spans]

Attention Deficit Disorder (ADD). The hallmark of an individual's mind being bombarded with entertaining bells and whistles, taking away any and almost all possible constructive, worthwhile progress that productive and driven-based people seemingly possess. A common neurodevelopmental disorder most frequently diagnosed in children. A disorder that, mind you, has been around for over 100 years, first being mentioned in 1902 by British pediatrician Sir George Frederic Still.[1] Though it seems, oddly enough, that the rise in cases seems to manifest sharply sometime in the early-'90s, which does —*bingo!*—fall under the current Millennial generation.

There are so many theories as to why this rise in ADD and, respectively, Attention Deficit Hyperactivity Disorder (ADHD) occurred. In the early 1990s, a seismic shift began to reshape our world: the rise of a digital playground. The advent of personal computers, the growing popularity of the internet, and the proliferation of video games heralded an era of unprecedented technological advancement. As screens infiltrated our daily lives, so too did a subtle but perceptible transformation in our collective attention spans. A study often cited in discussions about attention spans is from Microsoft Corporation, which found that the average human attention span decreased from 12-seconds in the year 2000 to 8-seconds in 2015, highlighting the impact of digital technology on our ability to focus.[2]

At the heart of this transformation was the burgeoning popularity of video games. For the first time, interactive digital environments captivated the imagination of millions: adults, a few elderly, and yes, the children who have now become the modern Millennials that they are. The arcade, once a refuge for pinball wizards in the '80s, was now a realm where players could navigate virtual worlds in the comfort of their own homes, battling foes and solving puzzles, all in dazzling 32-bit and 64-bit quality. These early forays into digital entertainment offered a tantalizing taste of the immersive experiences that would become ubiquitous in the decades to come.

Simultaneously, the World Wide Web emerged as a boundless repository of information, entertainment, and communication (i.e., AOL Instant Messenger, e-mail, and eventually social media sites like MySpace and Friendster). Suddenly, the answers to our questions were just a search query away. It made life faster and easier. Schoolwork changed completely with the library almost becoming completely obsolete overnight. The internet beckoned with its promise of instant access to knowledge, forging a new frontier in human connectivity. And we all knew it. . . . However, this newfound accessibility came at a cost—a gradual erosion of patience and sustained focus. And furthermore, a reduction in Critical Thinking. A study in JAMA Pediatrics reported that children who spend more than two hours a day on screens score lower on language and thinking tests, and children who spend more than seven hours a day on screens show a thinning of the brain's cortex, the area responsible for critical thinking and reasoning.[3]

The digital revolution was a multi-sensory affair. Screens bombarded us with a barrage of visual stimuli, accompanied by the cacophony of synthesized soundtracks and the tap-tap-tap of keyboards and controllers. For the first time ever, it actually felt as though we were experiencing a true connection with machines as we operated them seamlessly and naturally through our mind-to-controller linkage. This sensory overload, as groundbreaking and earth-shattering as it was, became a defining feature of the digital age, conditioning our brains to process information in rapid, bite-sized morsels rather than through prolonged, contemplative engagement. No longer were the days of slowing down, taking our time, and waiting for the gratification that was once worked for and relished by previous generations.

Video games, in particular, excelled at leveraging psychological principles to capture and retain attention. The incorporation of leveling systems, achievements, and unlockable content tapped into our innate desire for progress and mastery. With each accomplishment, a surge of dopamine—the brain's pleasure neurotransmitter—reinforced the cycle, fostering a sense of achievement that incentivized continued play, over and over and over again. And now, again—in the modern digital realm—content is boundlessly abundant but transient: Social media feeds, forums, and news sites offer a ceaseless stream of updates, each vying for a morsel of our attention. Our lives have become video games that we can't and do not care to escape.

The impermanence of online content instills a sense of urgency, encouraging rapid consumption and diminishing the inclination for sustained reflection. The hyperlink, a fundamental feature of web navigation, exemplifies the fractured nature of online attention. Clicking from one link to another, we traverse a vast digital landscape, flitting from topic to topic without the constraints of linear thought. While this nonlinear exploration can be intellectually enriching, it also fosters a propensity for distraction and skimming over depth. As technology advanced, so did our capacity—or perhaps compulsion—to multitask. Simultaneously juggling multiple digital interactions became the norm. We checked emails while browsing news articles, chatted on instant messengers while listening to music, and toggled between open windows with lightning speed. This culture of multitasking further divided our attention, fragmenting our focus across disparate tasks.

The early 1990s marked a pivotal juncture in our relationship with technology. The digital landscape that emerged brought unprecedented opportunities for connection, learning, and entertainment. Yet, in this whirlwind of innovation, our collective attention spans bore the subtle but indelible marks of change. The interplay of video games, the internet, and the evolving digital experience sculpted our cognitive landscape, ushering in an era defined by rapid information consumption and fleeting focus. A report by Common Sense Media found that teenagers spend an average of over 7-hours per day on screen media for entertainment, and children aged 8-12 spend about 5-hours on average. This does not include time spent on screens for educational purposes.[4] This is by far the most alarming fact on the subject, and this is not a good direction this generation is taking.

It seems no longer are the days of keeping your mind fixed on a single task for an extended period, savoring the depth and richness of sustained engagement. Instead, we find ourselves ensnared in a cycle of constant distraction, our attention fragmented and fleeting amidst the ceaseless barrage of digital stimuli. The allure of the digital realm, with its promises of instant gratification and endless novelty, has reshaped our cognitive habits, conditioning us to seek out quick hits of stimulation rather than investing in the slow, deliberate cultivation of focused attention. Digital media, while revolutionary in how we access information and entertainment, has also been linked to significant psychological effects. The near-constant engagement with screens has been shown to alter the brain's reward system, making individuals more susceptible to boredom when not engaged with digital devices. This shift has implications not only for attention spans but also for overall mental health, contributing to increased rates of anxiety and depression among Millennials.

Social media platforms, with their algorithms designed to capture and hold our attention spans, whilst simultaneously encouraging the switching of applications and search results, exacerbate the challenges to our focus in daily life. Research published in the Journal of Social and Clinical Psychology links high social media use to decreased attention spans and increased symptoms of ADHD among adolescents. The study suggests that the constant switching between platforms could contribute to attentional difficulties.[5]

These social media companies not only encourage rapid switching between pieces of content but also foster a culture of comparison and instant feedback, impacting self-esteem and real-world relationships. The pressure to remain constantly connected and the *fear of missing out* (FOMO) contribute further to the fragmentation of attention and a decrease in the quality of social interactions. Addressing these challenges requires a multi-faceted approach. Encouraging digital literacy and mindfulness can help individuals become more aware of their digital consumption patterns and their effects. Techniques such as digital detoxes, setting specific times for technology use, and engaging in activities that promote focus and patience can counteract the negative impacts.

Additionally, educational systems can adapt by incorporating teaching methods that foster deeper engagement and critical thinking, preparing students to navigate a digital world without sacrificing their ability to concentrate and reflect deeply. As we navigate the complexities of the digital age, it's crucial to seek a balance between harnessing the benefits of technology and preserving our cognitive well-being. By understanding the implications of our digital consumption habits and adopting strategies to mitigate their negative effects, we can foster a healthier, more mindful engagement with the digital world.

When we steer through the fast-paced world of technology, it's crucial to pause and think about how it's changing us—especially our ability to pay attention. Our journey isn't about giving up on technology entirely, but about finding a healthy balance. We're at a point where we need to be mindful about how we use our devices and the internet. It's not just about the fear of losing our focus to screens; it's about making a conscious effort to control how we let technology into our lives. This chapter/essay isn't a goodbye to deep thinking or long periods of concentration; instead, it's a wake-up call to strive for a middle ground. By being aware and making small changes in how we interact with technology, we can shape a future where we use it to our advantage—keeping our minds sharp and our attention spans intact. Let's not be remembered as the generation that lost the ability to concentrate, but as the ones who found a way to thrive amidst the buzz of the digital age.

Reader's Group Discussion Questions

- Considering the historical context provided, how do you think the rise of digital media has contributed to the increased diagnosis of attention deficit disorders?

- How do the engagement strategies used in video games affect our expectations for stimulation from non-digital experiences?

- How has the internet's structure, particularly the use of hyperlinks and social media feeds, changed the way we process information and focus?

- Share your thoughts on multitasking with digital devices. Do you believe it has a positive or negative impact on your productivity and attention span?

- Discuss the social and psychological implications of our reliance on screens for entertainment, communication, and information.

- What strategies can we employ to mitigate the negative impacts of technology on our attention spans while still benefiting from digital advancements?

Footnotes:

[1] Holland, Kimberly; Medically reviewed by White, Marney A., PhD, MS, Psychology. October 28th, 2021. *Healthline*. "The History of ADHD: A Timeline". https://www.healthline.com/health/adhd/history#1902

[2] Microsoft Corporation, "Attention spans," 2015

[3] JAMA Pediatrics, "Screen Time and the Developing Brain," 2019

[4] Common Sense Media, "The Common Sense Census: Media Use by Tweens and Teens," 2019

[5] Journal of Social and Clinical Psychology, "Social Media Use and Attention Deficit Hyperactivity Disorder Symptoms in Adolescents," 2020

["drugs & alcohol": why millennials *love* to use recreational substances]

The awesomeness of Alcohol and Drug use is by no means a new fad. Since the beginning of time, humans have been the ultimate experimenters. From the bewildering variety of plants to mystifying fungi, and even the deadliest poisons, our curiosity has often led us to dabble with substances we knew full well could be our undoing. It seems there's nothing too perilous or puzzling that we won't poke, prod, or taste at least once—just for the thrill of discovery. To put it simply: Humans have always loved to change or control reality—and what better way to do that than with readily available substances?

Recreational (or otherwise) use serves as a means of escape from the pressures and stresses of daily life. Whether grappling with academic demands, professional responsibilities, or personal challenges, drugs and alcohol offer temporary respite from anxiety, depression, and emotional turmoil. The euphoric effects of substances provide a welcome distraction and a momentary reprieve from reality, allowing users to momentarily forget their troubles and experience a sense of relaxation or euphoria. Substance use often occurs in social settings, where individuals seek to enhance social interactions, boost confidence, and alleviate social anxiety. Alcohol, in particular, is commonly consumed in social gatherings, parties, and nightlife venues, where its disinhibiting effects can facilitate bonding, camaraderie, and interpersonal connections. Similarly, certain drugs such as MDMA (ecstasy) or cocaine may be used to enhance sociability, increase energy levels, and foster a sense of euphoria and connection with others.

Some individuals may perceive recreational substances as enhancing their creativity, productivity, and performance in various domains. For example, artists, musicians, and writers may use drugs such as cannabis or psychedelics to unlock new insights, enhance sensory perception, and stimulate creative expression. Similarly, stimulant drugs like Adderall or cocaine may be used by students or professionals to increase focus, alertness, and productivity, albeit with potential risks and consequences. Recreational substance use can also serve as a form of self-medication or coping mechanism for individuals struggling with mental health issues, trauma, or unresolved emotional pain. Drugs and alcohol may temporarily alleviate sadness, loneliness, or emptiness, providing a temporary sense of relief or numbness. However, reliance on substances as a coping mechanism can lead to dependency, addiction, and exacerbation of underlying mental health conditions, ultimately hindering personal growth and well-being.

The perceived benefits and preferences associated with substance use can profoundly shape an individual's trajectory in life, influencing both success and failure across various domains. While some may find temporary relief from stress, anxiety, or depression through recreational substance use, these fleeting advantages are often eclipsed by the long-term risks and consequences inherent in such behavior. In moments of success, individuals may experience a temporary boost in mood, sociability, or performance, finding solace in the alleviation of immediate burdens. Social settings, in particular, become arenas where drugs and alcohol foster enhanced sociability, confidence, and interpersonal connections, facilitating moments of bonding and camaraderie.

Cognitive impairment, impaired judgment, and a heightened propensity for risky behaviors further underscore the detrimental effects of substance use, culminating in a cycle of negative consequences and missed opportunities. Prolonged substance use exacerbates underlying mental health conditions, perpetuating a cycle of anxiety and depression, and hindering personal growth and recovery efforts. Ultimately, while recreational substance use may promise temporary respite or perceived advantages, its allure is fleeting, with long-term risks overshadowing any short-term gains. Recognizing and understanding the underlying motivations and implications of substance use is imperative for fostering informed decision-making, promoting harm reduction strategies, and supporting individuals in achieving holistic well-being and genuine success in life.

Why exactly Millennials are partaking so heavily in drug and alcohol use is speculation. Theories stem from the generation's early roots all the way to modern day. The influence of peers and social circles is a powerful determinant of behavior, especially during adolescence and young adulthood.[1] The Millennial generation, characterized by its interconnectedness through social media, may experience heightened peer pressure in both physical and virtual spaces, potentially leading to increased experimentation with substances.

Maybe it could be coinciding with the rise in mental health disorders like depression and anxiety. According to the Nation Institute of Health: "Nearly half of Americans surveyed [in a 2021 study] reported recent symptoms of an anxiety or depressive disorder, and 10% of respondents felt their mental health needs were not being met. Rates of anxiety, depression, and substance use disorder have increased since the beginning of the pandemic."[2] Many Millennials entered adulthood during times of economic instability, characterized by financial crises and uncertain job markets. These stressors can lead individuals to turn to substances as a coping mechanism. And the pandemic doesn't seem to be the only catalyst. Both anxiety and depression among young adults in the US have been increasing[3] from 2005 to 2017 by 63%, and it is only getting worse. . . .

The Millennial generation has shown a heightened awareness of mental health issues, namely because of accessibility to other peers online who are dealing with similar issues, and the ability to use possibly unreliable resources such as WebMD, YouTube, Reddit, etc. While this heightened awareness of mental health appears to be a positive development in many ways, it also means that more individuals may be grappling with mental health challenges that may—or in some cases inevitably—cause them to turn to drugs and alcohol as a form of self-medication. These of course would be attempts to alleviate symptoms of anxiety, depression, or other mental health conditions, as these substances do seem to temporarily elevate these conditions in the short term, but in the long term almost always make the conditions unfortunately worse, causing a vicious cycle of substance abuse.

Shifts in societal attitudes towards drugs and alcohol may also play a role in the increase among Millennials. In some circles, there has been a normalization or even glorification of substance use, perpetuated by mainstream media portrayals and pop cultural influences: music, television, social media, celebrities, and even YouTube. This altered perception can make experimentation with drugs and alcohol seem more acceptable.

The COVID-19 pandemic has had a profound impact on people's lives globally, with Millennials being particularly affected in various aspects, including their consumption of drugs and alcohol. Death from substances and Alcohol increased, according to the results from JAMA, showing that after increasing around 2.2% per year over the previous two decades, deaths involving alcohol jumped 25.5% between 2019 to 2020, totaling 99,107 deaths.[4] The combination of lockdowns, social isolation, economic uncertainties, and a constant stream of unsettling news (especially news of loved ones passing due to COVID-19 itself) had led to significant changes in behavior and coping mechanisms among this generation.

During the pandemic, many Millennials found themselves turning to alcohol and drugs as a form of escapism from the monotony and stress of their new daily lives, according to a study from the National Library of Medicine which found that there was a 22.03% increase in alcohol use since the pandemic had began.[5] With bars, restaurants, and social venues closed, the consumption of alcohol didn't stop; it merely shifted settings, moving into homes where virtual happy hours and solo drinking became more common. The ease of access to alcohol through delivery services and the lack of a structured day contributed to an increase in consumption levels for some. Similarly, the use of recreational drugs saw changes during the pandemic. For some Millennials, the stress, anxiety, and depression brought on by the pandemic led to increased usage as a way to self-medicate and momentarily escape the pressing reality. Cannabis, in particular, saw a rise in use, possibly due to its legal status in many places and its perceived less harmful effects compared to other substances.[6] More than 3 in 4 adults (77%) say the future of our nation is a significant source of stress, up significantly from 2019 when 66% of adults said the same.[7] And more than 7 in 10 Americans (71%) say this is the lowest point in our nation's history that they can remember. In 2019, only 56% of Americans shared this sentiment.

The pandemic also spurred a wave of self-reflection among many Millennials, leading to a reevaluation of their substance use habits. The health crisis highlighted the importance of physical and mental well-being, prompting some to reduce their consumption of alcohol and drugs. This period has seen a growing interest in healthier lifestyles, with more individuals exploring alternatives to substance use, such as exercise, meditation, and picking up new hobbies that contribute to a sense of fulfillment and well-being. .... The social aspect of drug and alcohol use among Millennials also underwent a transformation. The pandemic limited physical social interactions, reducing peer pressure and social cues that often lead to substance use. This change provided an opportunity for some to break free from social consumption patterns and assess their relationship with substances in a more isolated setting.

The emergence of modern craft beer marks a significant shift in the brewing landscape, representing a departure from mass-produced beers and a return to artisanal, flavor-rich brews. This movement gained momentum in the late-20th century and has evolved into a cultural phenomenon. Millennials, known for their penchant for unique experiences and authenticity, have become a key demographic for the craft beer industry.

Craft beer's roots trace back to the late-20th century, when a wave of microbreweries and brewpubs started to challenge the dominance of major beer corporations. These establishments prioritized quality, flavor diversity, and small-batch production methods. The movement was fueled by a desire to break away from the standardized, often bland, offerings of big beer companies, whose current duopoly of Anheuser-Busch InBev and MillerCoors has taken 90% of the total market.[8] As the craft beer scene flourished, Millennials, with their affinity for exploration and individuality, became a natural audience, especially due to the allure of breaking away from mainstream Big Beer. This generation tends to value experiences over products, and craft beer aligns with this ethos by offering a vast array of distinctive flavors and brewing styles. The craft beer movement's emphasis on local ingredients and community connections also resonates with Millennials' interest in sustainability and supporting local businesses.

The rise of social media has played a pivotal role in connecting craft breweries with Millennial consumers. Platforms like Instagram and Untappd provide a space for beer enthusiasts to share their discoveries, creating a virtual community around craft beer culture. Brewers leverage these platforms to showcase their unique creations, engage with consumers, and build a loyal fan base.

Moreover, the craft beer movement aligns with Millennials' interest in authenticity and transparency. Craft breweries often emphasize the craftsmanship behind their products, sharing stories about the brewing process, the sourcing of ingredients, and the faces behind the brand. This transparency fosters a sense of connection and trust between the consumer and the brewery. The craft beer industry's willingness to experiment with unconventional ingredients and brewing techniques also appeals to Millennials' adventurous palates. From barrel-aged stouts to sour ales infused with exotic fruits, craft breweries continuously push the boundaries of traditional brewing, offering consumers an ever-expanding palette of flavors to explore.

The start of modern craft beer represents a departure from mainstream brewing practices, emphasizing quality, diversity, and a connection to local communities. Millennials, with their appreciation for unique experiences, authenticity, and community engagement, have become a central demographic for the craft beer movement. As this industry continues to evolve, its ability to cater to the preferences and values of Millennials ensures its enduring relevance in the dynamic landscape of beverage culture.

Millennials face a lot of stress and pressure, and it's no surprise many turn to drugs and alcohol to cope. These substances might offer a temporary escape and a way to connect with others or feel more creative. But really, this behavior often covers up deeper issues like pain, loneliness, or searching for what really makes life meaningful. The COVID-19 pandemic made things even harder, making everyone think more about how to truly be happy and strong in tough times. Now, we're at a point where we need to look beyond the quick fix of getting high or drunk to deal with problems. By being more understanding and supportive of each other, spreading the word about how to stay mentally healthy, and creating strong support networks, we can help Millennials face challenges without relying on substances. This way, they can find real happiness and purpose that lasts longer than the temporary buzz from drugs or alcohol.

Reader's Group Discussion Questions

- How does acknowledging the long history of substance use help us understand modern attitudes toward drugs and alcohol?

- In what ways do drugs and alcohol provide an escape from modern life's pressures? Are there healthier alternatives for dealing with them?

- How do social settings influence individual choices about drug and alcohol use, and how can we foster environments that discourage harmful consumption?

- Can the use of substances genuinely enhance creativity and productivity, or is this perception misguided?

- How does the use of substances as a coping mechanism for mental health issues affect long-term well-being?

- How have changing societal attitudes and peer influence affected Millennials' approach to drug and alcohol use?

- What lessons can be learned from the changes in substance use patterns during the COVID-19 pandemic, and how can these insights inform future public health strategies?

Footnotes:

[1] Science Direct Staff, 2024. *Science Direct.* "Peer Influence". https://www.sciencedirect.com/topics/psychology/peer-influence#:~:text=Peer influences, and social influences,oriented toward work and family.

[2] NIH Staff. September 28th, 2023. *NIH.* "Mental Health During the COVID-19 Pandemic". https://covid19.nih.gov/covid-19-topics/mental-health#:~:text=In a 2021 study, nearly,the beginning of the pandemic.

[3] Osorio, Emma Kauana; Hyde, Emily. *Ballard Brief.* December, 2021. "The Rise of Anxiety and Depression Among Young Adults in the United States". https://ballardbrief.byu.edu/issue-briefs/the-rise-of-anxiety-and-depression-among-young-adults-in-the-united-states

[4] White, A. M.; Castle, I. P.; Powell, P. A.; Hingson, R. W.; Koob, G. F. Alcohol-Related Deaths During the COVID-19 Pandemic. JAMA, 327(17), 1704–1706, 2022. PMID: 35302593

[5] National Library of Medicine, NIH. Addict Behav Rep. 2021 Dec; 14: 100388. Published online 2021 Oct 21. doi: 10.1016/j.abrep.2021.100388, https://www.ncbi.nlm.nih.gov/pmc/articles/PMC8664966/table/t0005/

[6] Dills, Angela, Sietse Goffard, Jeffrey Miron, and Erin Partin. "The Effect of State Marijuana Legalizations: 2021 Update," Policy Analysis no. 908, Cato Institute, Washington, DC, February 2, 2021. https://doi.org/10.36009/PA.908.

[7] American Psychological Association (A.P.A.), "Stress in America 2020: A National Mental Health Crisis," 2020

[8] Lynn, Barry C. December 26th, 2012. *Harvard Business Review.* "Big Beer, A Moral Market, and Innovation". https://hbr.org/2012/12/big-beer-a-moral-market-and-in

["are millennials having sex?": an inquiry into the struggles of dating, social interactions, and overall sexualities at play]

It's easy for everyone to place blame on any one singular thing, but when it comes to the battle of the sexes, this is especially true. Modern-day tech companies have single-handedly changed the face of what it means to date in this chaotic America we all currently are living in. So much so that invented concepts such as "ghosting," "roaching," and even obscure ones like "situationships" have come into existence. These are things that have existed in the past in one form or another, but were relatively frowned upon and socially damning to the point where virtually nobody did them—or at least it wasn't seen through the lens of the all-seeing inter-webs. The reality is that nobody did them because social media hadn't existed yet, so it was much easier to gently shame or make someone aware of their wrongdoings in regard to treating prospective people who like and/or want them. There was a level of decency. Now, in this crazy time, all of that is thrown out the window.

Navigating the dating scene as a Millennial can feel like wading through a bizarre quagmire filled with the confused, the broke, the heartbroken, and the downright creepy (with an overrepresentation of men who might better fit the description of "boys"). Many approach these individuals with disdain or outright frustration, yet sometimes, a sense of pity emerges. Is it possible that these less-than-desirable traits are not entirely their fault but rather a product of the culture they were born into? Let's take a closer look at each characteristic and explore this possibility:

While it isn't inherently bad to be a "horny" individual, it does become problematic when it comes to intent when dating. These apps like Bumble and Tinder, superficial as they are (with the swipe left and swipe right method of "yes" or "no"), seem to enhance our sexual urges and innate desire for novelty, purely by connecting with sexually like-minded individuals. After all, if two people, in theory, are looking through these apps and swipe right on each other through simply—and very passively—viewing each other's physical attractiveness or witty bios, it could therefore be easier for them to link together and live happily ever after, right? While this may sound great in theory, in practice these individuals are starting their relationship with one another on superficial terms: Appearance and online first impressions. This can easily devolve the relationship into one thing: Sex. That is the hard truth Millennials have come to terms with.

Success and wealth play a key role in relationships, whether we like it or not. This isn't solely because of the money or fortune that comes with the person; it is because success and wealth define the character of an individual—their work ethic, their values, how well-liked they are, how they are viewed by other people, maybe even how smart they are —or maybe how well they navigate life. Resources are a factor, of course, but for the most part success and wealth are desirable only because of the perceived traits that come along with it. Compared to the Silent Generation, Baby Boomers, and Generation X, Millennials only make up about 8.5% of the total wealth in America.[1]

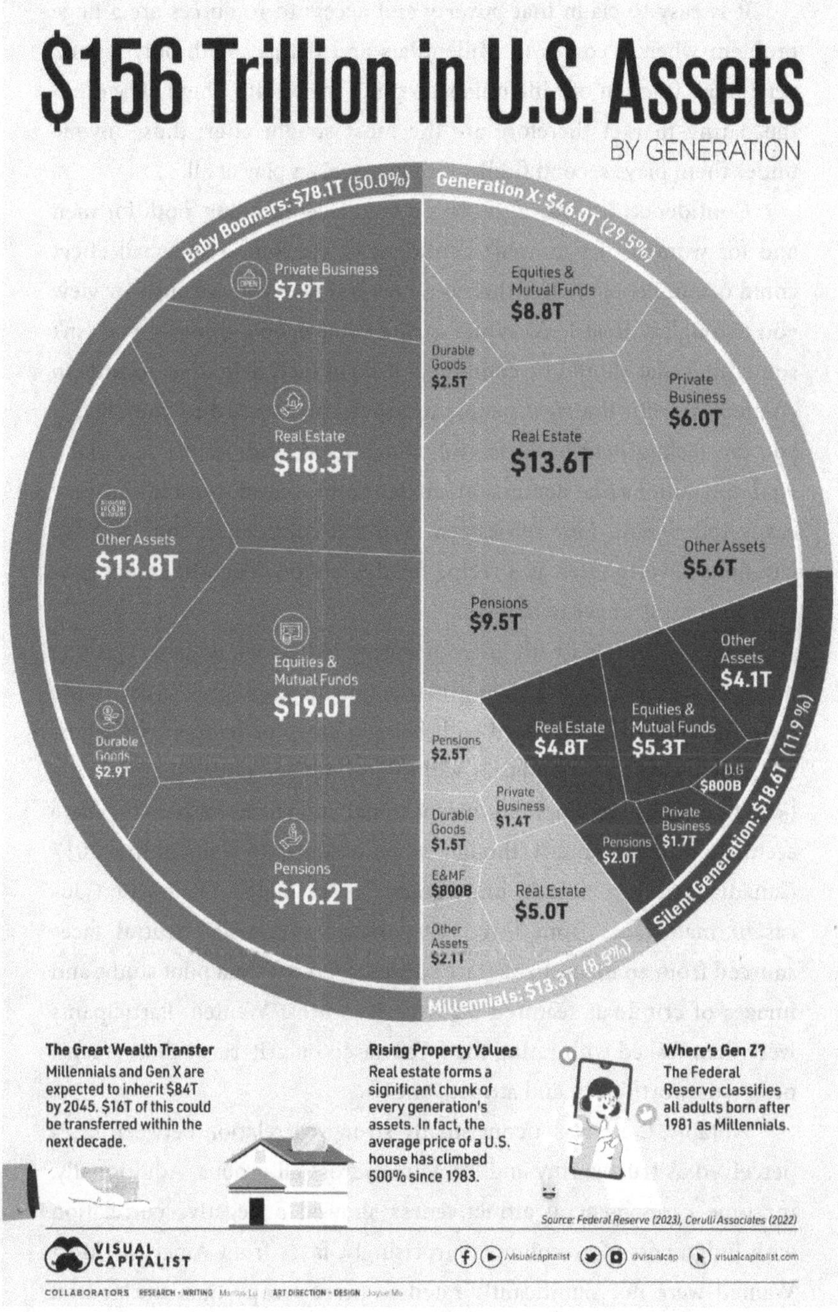

$156 Trillion in U.S. Assets
BY GENERATION

The Great Wealth Transfer

Millennials and Gen X are expected to inherit $84T by 2045. $16T of this could be transferred within the next decade.

Rising Property Values

Real estate forms a significant chunk of every generation's assets. In fact, the average price of a U.S. house has climbed 500% since 1983.

Where's Gen Z?

The Federal Reserve classifies all adults born after 1981 as Millennials.

Source: Federal Reserve (2023), Cerulli Associates (2022)

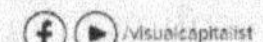  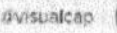 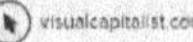

COLLABORATORS RESEARCH + WRITING Marcus Lu | ART DIRECTION + DESIGN Joyce Ma

It is easy to claim that poverty and access to resources are a huge problem when it comes to Millennials and dating. With only a very, very small fraction of Millennials carrying the wealth, these "1%ers" in the dating market therefore are the most sought after; thus, anyone under them plays second fiddle, if they can even play at all. . . .

Confidence, I think, also plays a vital role in dating, both for men and for women. If you aren't confident in yourself, a snowball effect could occur. People notice this, and may not take you seriously or view you through a great lens. While caring what people think of you isn't something that should be condoned, it is, in fact, helpful in regards to connecting with the *right* people to move you forward in your life. If you are feeling held back, fearful, squandered, and, dare I say, *like a victim*, emotions like depression, anxiety, and feeling tortured can very easily follow suit. Low self-esteem and self-confidence, coupled with climbing poverty rates, is a recipe for depression. The Millennial generation is no stranger to that fact.

Toxicity, coupled with gross or creepy behaviors, is the kryptonite of anyone in the digital dating market. In psychology, *disgust* is the only emotion well associated with being a creep or "creepy."[2] Disgust helps delineate the boundaries within and outside our bodies, serving both to establish and uphold interpersonal and social barriers.[3] There seems to be a disconnect, though, when it comes to women. In a 2017 Canadian study,[4] female undergraduates evaluated images of Caucasian male faces from three categories: emotionally neutral faces sourced from an image bank, faces deemed 'creepy' in a pilot study, and images of criminals featured on America's Most Wanted. Participants were then tasked with rating the faces based on criteria such as creepiness, trustworthiness, and attractiveness.

Notably, there was a consistently strong correlation between faces perceived as trustworthy and attractive across all groups. Additionally, in some cases, general attractiveness showed a negative correlation with judgments of creepiness. Surprisingly, faces from America's Most Wanted were not significantly rated as more creepy than the neutral group. Participants made rapid creepiness assessments, expressing high confidence in their judgments. For me, this is seen as a huge problem, mainly because actual creeps are possibly being overlooked and are replaced with possibly "benign" men. These men are the new crop in the dating market. Men who appeared disheveled and unkempt, those with abnormal facial features, and individuals aged between 31 and 50 were consistently rated as highly creepy.

Social awkwardness as it relates to social media has a consistent correlation. The primary connection between social anxiety disorder and social media lies in the reduced occurrence of in-person interactions.[5] While virtual interactions provide comfort for individuals with social anxiety, they can impede the individual's ability to engage with others face-to-face. In essence, the combination of social media usage, internet activity, a reluctance to engage in social networking, and a motivation to avoid in-person interactions is associated with heightened social anxiety. This assertion is substantiated by a 2015 study[6] examining the interplay between online and offline social behavior and its impact on the well-being of socially anxious adolescents and young adults. The study, involving 656 students, revealed that online social behavior correlated with lower well-being and increased social anxiety in offline social settings. This would explain why sociability among Millennials seems relatively low, and why more and more are complaining about things such as social awkwardness and social anxiety.[7] It's a merry-go-round loop of self-defeating single-ness (and therefore, the subsequent loneliness that comes with it).

But what exactly is the true crux of Millennials having lower sex rates than previous generations? Research indicates that Millennials and Gen-Z are experiencing a trend of increased sexual inactivity compared to previous generations.[8] The research found that individuals born in the 1980s and 1990s were more likely to report having no sexual partners as adults compared to those born in the 1960s and

1970s. Among those aged 20 to 24, more than twice as many Millennials born in the 1990s (15%) reported having no sexual partners since age 18 compared to Gen X-ers born in the 1960s (6%).[9]

Top of the list of reasons that Millennials are having lower sex rates, in my humble opinion, would have to be social media and online dating. With online dating becoming more and more prevalent, and less and less about connection and more and more about outward appearance, it is no wonder that men and women are competing against each other for the top-tier males and females. Males and females that are handsome/beautiful, rich and not poor (or even middle-class), taller and broader shoulders (among males), bigger breasts, wider hips, bigger tush (among females), and a wildly large social media presence (popularity). A new study, by scientists at the University of St Andrews, found that people with access to the internet preferred more masculine men and more feminine and thinner women.[10] Clout, status, and attractiveness have warped what it means to date for a connection. And when the media, movies, magazines, friends and family, and even sometimes employment favors such characteristics in a person, this can make one strive for something that they may not be aware is close to impossible, such as gaining the attention of a male or female with thousands upon thousands of matches in their dating feed.

A personal anecdote of mine comes from a Tinder date I experienced. Tinder, a prevalent online dating application, is notorious for burgeoning the insipid online hookup culture of empty, meaningless sex. Admittedly, I partook in it after a rather ugly breakup in the Summer of 2015, going through as many women as I could in order to fill an emptiness within me. Like so many Millennials, this is something that is not an uncommon experience. . . . But there was one date, in particular, that stroke a nerve in me—and obviously compelled me to mention it in a book! . . . To keep her real name anonymous, let's say her name is "L."

As I was swiping left and right on my Tinder dashboard, I came across L. She was a gorgeous, adventurous, fit, and extremely healthy woman in her early-'20s—maybe even 18 or 19. There was no way I would match with her, I thought . . . but sure enough, I actually did. We messaged back and forth, hit it off (virtually), and both decided to schedule a date at the beach. During our date, after eating lunch, we sat near the shore, looking up at the bright blue sky and discussing things about ourselves in detail—the normal first date conversations of pasts, where from, etc. At some point in the conversation, we got to talking about Tinder, and how horrible of an app it is . . . ironically. I told her my thoughts about it, and she mostly agreed . . . but then said something about it that I thought was so peculiar:

"I mostly don't like Tinder because of how . . . well, *infinite* it is!"

Infinite? I didn't understand what L had meant. So I asked her, and she proceeded to pull out her phone to show me. What I saw on L's feed was not the normal way that (at least men) view Tinder. Firstly, she had Tinder Plus, a paid-for subscription within the app, which amplifies the likelihood of matches, plus other features included. (At the time, I had it as well.) But what was alarming was that she wasn't using her regular dashboard like I had. It never occurred to her to use that method. She actually went into the rare button in the bottom center that I rarely, if ever, pressed—mostly because it wouldn't ever be relevant to me. . . . . It was the *people-you-already-matched-with* button. When she pressed it, what I saw at the top of her screen was "999+," and then in the middle of her screen a profile of a random handsome dude that she could choose to swipe right on (to match with him), or left on (to kick him to the curb, regardless if he already liked her or not). The cherry-on-top for me was that she had so many men (and probably women) liking her that the app's numeration limitations couldn't give her a real number: "999+."

While this may sound conceded on L's part to show me this, she was very much a sweetheart about it, and truly thought that everyone who used the app experienced this level of god-like matches. The way she used Tinder was basically what everyone who has used or has ever used the app would dream of. . . . A bevy of suitable people who already liked you, and you simply swipe right or left on what you want or don't want, effectively doing no wondering, no work. True, blissful, worry-free dating. Take your pick. The world is your oyster. . . .

This, initially, gave me a huge ego boost, because my rationale was that if there were *that* many matches on her feed, then that would mean that I not only got her to swipe right and match with me, but I was actually charming enough to go on a first date with her too! But it also made me wonder if most beautiful women experienced this. Coming from a truly sweet and innocent woman who thought it was this way for everyone, I got an insight into her world, and it made me ponder just how privileged she was as far as the dating market was concerned. She was the top 1% that everyone was competing for. And that was when I understood that almost all of those "999+" men and women will have a tiny sliver of a chance with this girl. That is the reality and the common theme in the current dating market. If a prospective Millennial doesn't obtain L—or any of the seemingly endless other "L's" out there—this could lead to that Millennial becoming depressed, chronically single, giving up in the dating market, etc.

For any rational person who views this experience I had with a sane head, this seems relatively ridiculous, as it seems like dating should be about connection, trust, and actual compromise and love—however, the reality is that this simply is not the case. All of these dating apps (Tinder, Bumble, Hinge, POF, et cetera) run on an algorithm to keep users hooked. The top way of doing that is to put the most-liked male or female at the very top of a new user's feed when they open the app, and occasionally place them, a new user, at the top of the well-liked individual's feed, throwing a bone every now and then of a high-tier match. It makes the new user *feel good*. Endorphins. Excitement. It makes the user find and feel what success is like in the dating market, regardless if an actual date arises or comes to fruition. And that feeling directly impacts how they view the opposite sex.

The chase then becomes the 1%, as opposed to who actually is *right for you*. This trend can lead to a so-called "dodging effect" of suitable lovers that may result in a successful relationship and genuine happiness. Effectively, these apps are putting actual dating at the wayside. When two people are matching based on looks, there is a sliding scale of the user's effective likability, statistics, and level of attractiveness that is in the background. This recipe accelerates superficial dating, and, likely, the subsequent devolvement of hookup culture.

The apparent contradiction between the lower sex rates among Millennials compared to previous generations and the prominent hookup culture within both Millennials and Gen-Zers poses a complex puzzle. This discrepancy may highlight an emerging stratification within the Millennial group, suggesting a division based on sexual activity levels. On one hand, there is a theory that sexual dynamics are influenced by differing capabilities and preferences between genders: men traditionally initiate and pursue, while women hold the decisive power in consenting to sexual engagements. This dynamic suggests that only a select group of men—those with perceived higher status due to wealth, appearance, or other desirable traits—achieve sexual success, yet may not find genuine emotional connection.

On the other hand, there's a theory that a diminished valuation of sex, spurred by negative personal experiences or societal factors (an ugly breakup, not attaining self-love, depression, anxiety, and/or substance abuse—including drinking), leads to indiscriminate sexual encounters among those who share this disenchantment. However, it's important to acknowledge a segment of Millennials who maintain traditional views on love and sex, or who abstain due to fear or personal choice, affecting overall sexual activity statistics. This situation underscores the diverse attitudes towards sex and intimacy within the generation, contributing to the observed paradox of reduced sex rates amidst a prevalent hookup culture.

Overall, there is no shame in not having sex—or having little amounts of sex. Sex has been and always will be a personal thing for everyone. Whether rich or poor, handsome or not, pretty or ugly, tall or short, fat or skinny, everyone has a say in what to do with their bodies. Millennials shouldn't be shamed for having lower sex, but it should be noted and explored to understand why it is that way.

Maybe having less sex is a silver lining. Less disease, better choices, fewer unwanted pregnancies, more focus on things that matter to the person, more time spent with friends and family, et cetera. Dating, at the end of the day, is just a means to get to know someone for who they are, and if you both mesh well, then mutually each person can—and should—be in each other's lives as a trusted partner.

If you do have no-strings-attached sex for pure entertainment or pleasure, though, please be safe and use protection. Sex is fun. Sex is great. But sex is not the end all, be all. What comes with it often is heartbreak, shame, or regret. That's not to say it is 100% always that way: It often is great when you do it with the right person—zero negatives involved, only positives. Someone you love and care for; someone who loves and cares for you back. That type of love makes the intimacy in question much more fulfilling. That's what we all *strive* for. That's what every generation strives for.

Reader's Group Discussion Questions

- The chapter discusses how modern dating apps and social media have transformed the dating landscape for Millennials. In what ways do you believe technology has positively or negatively affected the dynamics of dating and relationships? Share personal experiences or observations that support your views.

- "Ghosting," "roaching," and "situationships" are terms that have arisen with the evolution of digital dating. Discuss the impact of these phenomena on the emotional well-being of individuals involved. Have you or someone you know experienced these? What were the outcomes and lessons learned?

- The concept of "sexual market value" is subtly critiqued in the chapter, suggesting that people are often judged based on superficial traits such as wealth, appearance, and social media presence. How does this affect the self-esteem and dating behaviors of individuals? Discuss the difference between perceived value and real value in the context of personal relationships.

- The chapter proposes that decreased rates of sexual activity among Millennials might be linked to broader societal and personal issues, such as mental health and self-esteem. Discuss the potential connection between these factors. How do societal pressures and personal experiences converge to influence an individual's sexual choices and behaviors?

- The author introduces a personal anecdote to illustrate the disparities in dating experiences between individuals. Reflect on the story of "L" and the concept of the "dating market." How does this narrative align with or differ from your own dating experiences or those of people you know? Discuss the implications of believing that "the world is your oyster" in the context of dating.

- Finally, the chapter ends on a note that challenges the emphasis on sexual activity, suggesting that there are benefits to having less sex, such as fewer unwanted pregnancies and diseases, and more time for personal growth and relationships. Discuss the validity and implications of this perspective.

Footnotes:

---

[1] Lu, Marcus. August 17th, 2023. Visual Capitalist. "Visualizing $156 Trillion in U.S. Assets, by Generation". https://www.visualcapitalist.com/us-wealth-by-generation/

[2] Phillips ML, Senior C, Fahy T, David AS. Disgust – the forgotten emotion of psychiatry. British Journal of Psychiatry. 1998;172(5):373-375. doi:10.1192/bjp.172.5.373 - https://www.cambridge.org/core/journals/the-british-journal-of-psychiatry/article/disgust-the-forgotten-emotion-of-psychiatry/4888A05C20C78AF6523C5EC9D24A9DE4

[3] McAuliffe, K. (n.d.). "How disgust made humans cooperate to build civilisations." Aeon, June 6th, 2016. Retrieved from https://aeon.co/essays/how-disgust-made-humans-cooperate-to-build-civilisations.

[4] Watt, M. C., Maitland, R. A., & Gallagher, C. E. (2017). A case of the "heeby jeebies": An examination of intuitive judgements of "creepiness". Canadian Journal of Behavioural Science / Revue canadienne des sciences du comportement, 49(1), 58–69. https://doi.org/10.1037/cbs0000066

[5] Lee, B., & Stapinski, L. (2012). Seeking safety on the internet: relationship between social anxiety and problematic internet use.. *Journal of anxiety disorders*, 26 1, 197-205 . https://doi.org/10.1016/j.janxdis.2011.11.001.

[6] Koo HJ, Woo S, Yang E, Kwon JH. The Double Meaning of Online Social Space: Three-Way Interactions Among Social Anxiety, Online Social Behavior, and Offline Social Behavior. Cyberpsychol Behav Soc Netw. 2015 Sep;18(9):514-20. doi: 10.1089/cyber.2014.0396. PMID: 26348811.

[7] Jefferies, P., & Ungar, M. (2020). Social anxiety in young people: A prevalence study in seven countries. *PLoS ONE*, 15. https://doi.org/10.1371/journal.pone.0239133.

[8] Twenge, J., Sherman, R., & Wells, B. (2017). Sexual Inactivity During Young Adulthood Is More Common Among U.S. Millennials and iGen: Age, Period, and Cohort Effects on Having No Sexual Partners After Age 18. *Archives of Sexual Behavior*, 46, 433-440. https://doi.org/10.1007/s10508-016-0798-z.

[9] *It should be noted, though, that this trend was more pronounced among women and was absent among African Americans and those with a college education. The study utilized the General Social Survey, a nationally representative sample of American adults, to examine these trends, highlighting a shift towards higher rates of sexual inactivity among younger generations.*

[10] University of St. Andrews Staff Writer. July 11th, 2014. *Medical Xpress*. "The internet influences what people think is attractive in others, according to new research". https://medicalxpress.com/news/2014-07-internet-people.html

["pornography": why is it killing us?]

Possibly the most alarming statistic that I have seen in regards to erotic adult content, is the fact that 12% of all websites on the entire internet are pornography.[1] A close second would have to be that it is viewed by approximately 69% of American men and 40% of American women in any given year.[2] With that amount of viewership, it is no surprise that in 2023 the Adult & Pornographic Websites industry in the United States was on track to match the revenue of the National Collegiate Athletic Association (NCAA) at $1.15 billion.[3] The reason I bring forth all of these numbers is to showcase to you just how colossal, however obvious though it may be, of an entity the adult entertainment industry is in our lives—namely on the lives of Millennials and Gen-Zers.

There is no question that sex sells. It always has and always will. Humans are drawn to sex like a magnet. Advertising, the media, and the corporate world take full advantage of it, crafting campaigns that are both subtle and overt in their approach. From the billboards that dot highways showcasing scantily clad models to the commercials that pepper our television viewing, featuring innuendos and suggestive content, the strategy is clear and effective. This isn't a new phenomenon;

the use of sexual imagery to attract attention and sell products has a long and varied history, stretching back to the early days of advertising itself. The allure of sex appeal in advertising taps into basic human instincts—desire, curiosity, and attraction. Psychologically, these elements are powerful drivers of human behavior, influencing decisions and preferences often on a subconscious level. Advertisers are keenly aware of this dynamic and leverage it to create connections between a brand and its target audience. The promise of sex appeal, even when obliquely suggested, can enhance a product's perceived value, making it more desirable to consumers.

Pornography, on the other hand, represents a more direct and explicit exploration of human sexuality, standing apart from the subtleties of sex in mainstream advertising. While advertising employs sex appeal to suggest and entice, pornography offers an unambiguous depiction of sexual acts and fantasies. This distinction is crucial in understanding the broader implications of sex in media and advertising. The proliferation of pornography, especially with the advent of the internet, has led to significant discourse on its impact on society. Critics argue that engaging with pornography not only correlates with a decrease in sexual life satisfaction among individuals[4], but it also markedly fuels an increased appetite for rough or violent sexual experiences.[5] Moreover, this pattern of consumption is intricately linked with heightened probabilities of marital discord, ultimately paving the way for a twofold rise in divorce rates—up to and especially when people start watching pornography.[6] This phenomenon points to a deeper, more complex relationship between personal satisfaction, desires, and the stability of intimate relationships, revealing the multifaceted and often hidden repercussions of pornography on the fabric of human connections.

The ethical considerations surrounding pornography are complex and multifaceted. A study from the Journal of Behavioral Addictions in 2019 reported that when asked directly, only 14% of Americans agreed or strongly agreed that pornography was morally wrong, as compared to 51% who disagreed or strongly disagreed with that sentiment.[7] Issues such as consent, exploitation, and the potential for addiction are at the forefront of debates. Furthermore, the accessibility of pornography raises concerns about its exposure to minors and the shaping of young people's attitudes toward sex and consent. Psychologically, the consumption of pornography can have varied effects on individuals. While it can serve as a source of education and empowerment for some, for others, it may lead to issues with sexual satisfaction, relationship dynamics, and even mental health challenges. The impact is often influenced by factors such as frequency of consumption, the nature of the content viewed, and an individual's pre-existing attitudes toward sex.

Millennials, in particular, and in the context of social media and collective views of sex, find themselves at a unique crossroads. The digital age has ushered in an unprecedented level of access to sexual content, shaping perceptions and expectations of sex in profound ways. For many in this generation, pornography has become a primary source of sexual education, due in part to the lack of comprehensive sex education in schools and the stigma that still surrounds open discussions about sex. This reality has led to a gap in understanding about healthy sexual relationships, consent, and sexual health.

Social media further complicates the landscape by blurring the lines between private and public spheres, allowing for the widespread sharing of sexualized content. The normalization of such content on platforms frequented by Millennials and Gen-Zers contributes to an environment where sexual expression and exploration are more visible and, in some ways, more accepted.[8] However, this visibility often comes with its own set of challenges, including the pressure to conform to unrealistic body standards and sexual practices that are frequently portrayed in both pornography and sexualized advertising.

The implications of these dynamics are far-reaching. On one hand, the greater openness towards discussing sex could lead to more progressive attitudes towards sexual health and consent. On the other hand, the pervasive presence of pornography and sexualized images in media and advertising may reinforce harmful stereotypes and expectations. The challenge for society, then, is to navigate these complexities in a way that promotes healthy attitudes towards sex while addressing the potential negative impacts of its omnipresence in media and online.

Setting aside the internet and social media, porn has been proven to diminish romantic relationships between couples in many ways. While it's important to recognize that effects can vary significantly between different couples and individuals, there are several common issues reported in studies and clinical observations.

Unrealistic expectations, as a start, can be a significant problem. Pornography often portrays sexual activity in a way that is not representative of real intimate encounters. This can lead to unrealistic expectations regarding physical appearance, sexual performance, and what constitutes 'normal' sexual activities. When individuals expect their partners to mirror what they see in porn, it can plant seeds of dissatisfaction and inadequacy in a relationship, eroding the bedrock of mutual respect and pleasure. When real intimate encounters don't measure up to these fabricated standards, it can leave partners feeling pressured and disappointed.

Another issue is the potential for decreased sexual satisfaction. Regular consumption of pornography can alter an individual's perception of sex and intimacy, leading to decreased interest in and satisfaction with real-life sexual encounters. This can be due to desensitization, where more extreme or varied content becomes necessary for arousal, making regular intimate experiences seem less exciting or fulfilling. This shift can cause a rift between partners, as one may become more focused on the fantasy world of pornography than on the real-life relationship.

Furthermore, secrecy or deceit surrounding pornography use can erode trust within a relationship. If one partner is using porn frequently and hiding it from the other, it can lead to feelings of betrayal, jealousy, and insecurity. This is particularly the case if the use of pornography is considered a breach of the relationship's boundaries or agreements. The discovery of such activities can lead to conflict, a breakdown in communication, and a weakening of the partnership's foundation. Additionally, there is the issue of emotional disconnection. Engaging with pornography can become a substitute for genuine intimacy and connection, leading individuals to withdraw emotionally from their partner. This can result in a lack of emotional availability, as the individual may become more invested in the fantasy relationships portrayed in porn than in their real-life relationship. Over time, this can create a significant emotional gap between partners, reducing the quality and depth of the relationship.

The truest and most depraved form of pornography is in its infancy, but is swiftly, like all technologies, growing in sophistication—and it is coming our way faster than we realize.

Virtual Reality (VR) and Artificial-Intelligence (AI) generated imagery will inevitably be all the rage when it comes to porn consumption. The idea of putting on your Oculus Rifts, Meta Quests, Playstation VRs, and your Apple Vision Pros, and diving headfirst into a virtual brothel of alluring and nude women (or men) is not far off from our horizon. The implications of such technology are something that none of us could predict. What will it do to us mentally? What changes to dating will it make? And what if they may make it so enticing and so pleasurable to the point that actual human touch becomes second fiddle?

The possibility of preferring programmed pleasure over human connection poses a significant shift in how future generations perceive intimacy. The convenience and accessibility of AI-driven virtual experiences might lead to a devaluation of genuine human interactions, altering the very fabric of how relationships are formed and maintained. This shift could also impact the development of social skills among younger generations, who might find themselves more comfortable in virtual realms than in physical social settings. The seductive allure of a virtual world where every fantasy can be realized not only raises questions about the future of human intimacy but also about the ethical considerations of such profound escapism.

VR and AI in adult content introduce an unprecedented level of user immersion. This technological advancement is poised to significantly impact users' psychological well-being, potentially amplifying existing issues like social withdrawal, depression, and unrealistic sexual expectations. As individuals increasingly turn to these sophisticated virtual experiences for comfort, the disparity between the virtual simplicity and the complexity of actual human interactions may lead to heightened dissatisfaction and isolation. This raises critical questions: How will our mental health support frameworks adapt to tackle these novel forms of addiction and alienation? Are there ethical approaches to prevent or mitigate these potential harms? Moreover, the advent of VR and AI in this context brings to light complex ethical questions, particularly concerning the portrayal of acts that are considered illegal or morally reprehensible in the real world. Should these acts be permissible in a virtual setting if they do not harm real individuals, or do they still pose a risk by potentially warping a user's perception and behaviors in harmful ways? These are challenges we must confront as these technologies evolve.

As VR becomes more advanced and immersive, so too does the challenge of regulating its content. Creation of lifelike simulations for sexual gratification presents vast ethical challenges, including issues of consent, exploitation, and the potential normalization of harmful behaviors. The accessibility of these technologies to minors and their impact on young people's understanding of intimacy and consent is a pressing issue that demands our attention. Policymakers face a significant task in navigating these concerns, aiming to establish regulations that reflect and uphold the moral and ethical standards of our society.

Deepfakes, commonly referred to as synthetic media, utilize AI and machine learning techniques to create or manipulate video and audio recordings that appear genuinely real. This technology enables the alteration of existing images, videos, or audio clips to produce realistic, yet entirely fabricated, content. Initially emerging from deep learning practices, deepfakes have gained notoriety for their potential use in creating misleading media, impersonating individuals, and spreading widespread disinformation.

The creation of deepfakes involves training AI algorithms, typically through methods such as Generative Adversarial Networks (GANs), where two neural networks work against each other: one generates the fake content, while the other attempts to detect its authenticity. Over time, this process refines the output, resulting in increasingly convincing fakes. Eventually, as we know that technology is always and forever advancing, AI will have nearly perfected deepfakes to the point where detecting them is nearly impossible. The implications of deepfake technologies are widespread, affecting fields such as politics, entertainment, and personal security.

Politically, deepfakes can be used to undermine public figures by simulating controversial statements or actions that never occurred—visa-versa, the very knowledge the public eye has about deepfakes could be a politician's perfect excuse for why the video is false or misleading. "That isn't me!" the politician says. "Clearly, my opponent created it to damn my image and my campaign for president!" Meanwhile, it could be possible the video/audio of them was, in fact, genuine, but the sophistication of deepfakes in the future will blur the lines between what is true and what is false. This power alone is going to ramp up huge division within parties, and the average voter, when realizing deepfakes and their power, will not know how to effectively vote if they do not know what is actually being said by the candidate they are looking to maybe vote for. This is beyond terrifying. . . .

In entertainment, deepfakes raise ethical concerns regarding consent and the portrayal of celebrities in fictional scenarios. The best example comes from the creators of South Park, Matt Stone and Trey Parker (along with Peter Serafinowicz), who made a comedic web series on YouTube entitled "Sassy Justice,"[9] which premiered on October 26, 2020. The show utilizes deepfake technology to feature celebrities and politicians in the fictional world of TV reporter Fred Sassy from Cheyenne, Wyoming. Fred Sassy is physically acted by Trey Parker, and the deepfake face over his acting footage is the actual face of the 45th president of the United States, Donald J. Trump.

The show delves into issues like media manipulation and fake news, with Fred Sassy investigating the news itself. In particular, the first episode features another deepfake of Al Gore, a political figure Trey Parker and Matt Stone often poke fun at within South Park, who goes on to tell Fred Sassy that there is a deepfake video of Tom Cruise floating around, and how much of an issue deepfake technology is on our way of life. Ironically, the comedic part of it, of course, is that the entire show is all deepfakes. This is their bit. But interestingly, an actual Tom Cruise viral video fooled[10] the likes of many TikTok users:

> In some now-deleted TikToks, user @deeptomcruise released a trio of slightly disturbing videos. They're Tom Cruise look-alikes, talking and acting like the celebrity, with just the smallest hints that the face isn't real. Slight distorting, the face not working behind sunglasses as well, and the deadness of the eyes make it so that it's not 100% Tom, but if you saw one of these clips in passing, you might not think twice about the clip being edited at all.

From the standpoint of personal security, deepfakes pose significant risks, including fraud, identity theft, and character assassination. The most alarming scenario involves you, the reader—yes, that's right, you! As this technology advances, anyone could potentially misuse your appearance, voice, or other personal data to forge audio or video clips. This could lead to various forms of exploitation or defamation, tarnishing your relationships, finances, career, or online reputation. They could even produce inappropriate content, such as pornographic material, using your likeness. This is both unsettling and repugnant. So much so that even the United Kingdom has outright criminalized the creation of sexually explicit deepfake images.[11] As the technology becomes more advanced, distinguishing these forgeries from your real actions could become impossible.

As deepfake technology progresses, it becomes increasingly difficult to tell authentic from fabricated content, which raises profound questions about truth, trust, and objective reality in the digital age. This underscores the urgent need for comprehensive legal, technical, and ethical measures to counteract the proliferation of deepfake materials. It remains uncertain whether the speed at which deepfake technology achieves realism will match the technology needed to combat it.

Pornography and its many dangers are well-known. Ultimately, it is up to the person in question to decide if they will partake in its recreation, or abstain from it and its potential harms outlined in this chapter/essay. Like any addictive substance (prescription, illegal, depraved, or otherwise), there are supposed "benefits" and there are possibly (and almost always) unwanted side effects, some of which are catastrophic. Millennials and Gen-Zers, please heed this warning: This level of realism and pleasure derived from advancing sexual technology is something that we do not yet understand the long-term implications of as a human society. Be careful and tread lightly.

Reader's Group Discussion Questions

- This chapter presents staggering statistics about the prevalence of pornography on the internet and its viewership among Americans. How do these figures impact your understanding of the influence of pornography in society? Discuss any surprises or confirmations these statistics provide about current trends.

- The author discusses the dual role of sex in advertising and pornography, highlighting the differences in how each uses sexual content to attract attention. How do you perceive the impact of these two forms of media on societal norms and individual behaviors?

- Reflect on the ethical considerations mentioned regarding pornography, including consent, exploitation, and addiction. How do these issues align with or challenge your own views on the morality and consumption of pornographic content?

- The text explores the significant effects of pornography on relationships, citing problems like unrealistic expectations and decreased sexual satisfaction. Share your thoughts or experiences on how media portrayals of sex, not limited to pornography, can influence real-life relationships and personal contentment.

- The chapter delves into the emerging technologies of VR and AI in the context of adult content. Discuss the potential societal and individual implications of these advancements. Do you believe that technology is outpacing our ability to understand and regulate its effects on human intimacy and relationships?

- Finally, the chapter concludes with a cautionary note to Millennials and Gen-Zers regarding the uncharted territory of sexual technology and its realism. What measures, if any, do you think could be implemented to mitigate the potential harms discussed? Reflect on the balance between freedom of expression and the protection of societal welfare.

Footnotes:

[1] Faraz Ahmed, M. Zubair Shafiq, and Alex X. Liu, "The Internet is For Porn: Measurement and Analysis of Online Adult Traffic," 2016 IEEE 36th International Conference on Distributed Computing Systems (2016): 88, https://doi.org/10.1109/ICDCS.2016.81.

[2] Mark Regnerus, David Gordon, and Joseph Price, "Documenting Pornography Use in America: A Comparative Analysis of Methodological Approaches," The Journal of Sex Research 53, no. 7 (2016): 873–81, https://doi.org/10.1080/00224499.2015.1096886.

[3] "Adult & Pornographic Websites in the US - Market Size 2005–2028," IBISWorld, June 18, 2022, https://my.ibisworld.com/us/en/industry-specialized/od4576/industry-performance#current-performance.

[4] Daniel A. Cox, Beatrice Lee, and Dana Popky, "Politics, Sex, and Sexuality: The Growing Gender Divide in American Life," Survey Center on American Life, April 27, 2022, https://www.americansurveycenter.org/research/march-2022-aps/.

[5] Emily A. Vogels and Lucia F. O'Sullivan, "The Relationship Among Online Sexually Explicit Material Exposure To, Desire For, and Participation in Rough Sex," Archives of Sexual Behavior 48, no. 2 (2019): 653–65, https://doi.org/10.1007/s10508-018-1290-8.

[6] David Shultz, "Divorce Rates Double When People Start Watching Porn," Science, August 26, 2016, https://www.science.org/content/article/divorce-rates-double-when-people-start-watching-porn#:~:text=Analyzing%20the%20data%2C%20Perry%20and,from%206%5%20to%2018%25.

[7] J. B. Grubbs, S. W. Kraus, and S. L. Perry, "Self-Reported Addiction to Pornography in a Nationally Representative Sample: The Roles of Use Habits, Religiousness, and Moral Incongruence," Journal of Behavioral Addictions 8, no. 1 (2019): 88–93, https://doi.org/10.1556%2F2006.7.2018.134.

[8] Kaviani, C., & Nelson, A. (2020). Smartphones and the sexual behaviour of Generation Z college men in the USA. *Sex Education*, 21, 378 - 385. https://doi.org/10.1080/14681811.2020.1790350.

[9] Youtube User: Sassy Justice. Published October 26th, 2020. *Youtube.com*. "Sassy Justice with Fred Sassy (Full Episode) | Deep Fake and Deep Fake: The Movie". https://www.youtube.com/watch?v=9WfZuNceFDM

[10] Mellor, Imogen. March, 2021. *Gaming Bible*. "Bizarre Tom Cruise Deepfake Videos Are Being Linked To South Park Creators". https://www.gamingbible.com/news/games-bizarre-tom-cruise-deepfake-videos-are-being-linked-to-south-park-20210303

[11] TIME Staff. April 15th, 2024. *TIME*. "U.K. to Criminalize Creating Sexually Explicit Deepfake Images". https://time.com/6967243/uk-criminalize-sexual-explicit-deepfake-images-ai/

["the rise of OnlyFans": a get-rich-quick dilemma, women's empowerment, and modern entitlement]

For women born with conventional beauty and gifted genetics, the world is given to them on a silver platter. . . . While it may be a total eye-roll for those coming to terms with this fact, it is still a universal truth around the world—and probably by design. . . . If a God does exist, though, He most certainly chose to make everyone unequal. Or better yet, He made everyone so radically different that humans them*selves* have devised a greater goal of keeping those they deem lesser than them completely under their thumb . . . *for always and eternity*. And women's beauty is marked in this mindset as the highest ideal. . . .

For anyone in power, anyone who is poor, lonely, distraught, or even just average—almost everyone on the planet craves a level of beauty. We cannot objectively come to an agreement with what beauty is or even what it isn't (sometimes, for the most part)—but we objectively all know that beauty does exist and is here to stay for as long as humans walk the earth.

The debate I bring forth as it pertains to women's beauty isn't so much what is the universal list of characteristics that we can define as "beautiful" or "ideal"—because we all know, obviously, that they are not quantifiable. I more want to cover what women's beauty means and how much it influences our daily American lives, on a micro- or macro-level, unconsciously or subconsciously, and at what depths. . . . At the heart of this debate lies the pervasive influence of beauty standards on every facet of society, particularly within the context of modern American culture. From media representations and advertising campaigns to interpersonal relationships and professional opportunities, the idealization of beauty permeates our collective consciousness, shaping perceptions of self-worth, success, and social status.[1]

To quantify the "level of attractiveness" (LOA) of a female would require an impossible pursuit: Taking all individuals, males and females, on the planet and one by one having each individual, somehow without bias, rate each female on a scale from 1 to 10 and then collect together those answers and average them for each and every female. This average from all people on the planet would create the resulting LOA for that female. It would be hard to quantify—and much harder to find perfect 10s or perfect 1s. My prediction would be *a bell curve of beauty*, so to speak. But setting aside the notion of this thought experiment, it would be curious to assume if the females with this supposed attractive edge would see other statistics in their lives going up along with their LOA, as well. In this hypothetical graph, the higher the female's average number, so, too, would her average estimated income, perceived likability, self-esteem, self-graded mental health level, and overall well-being. . . .

For women born with conventional beauty and gifted genetics, the privileges afforded by society often come at the expense of perpetuating unrealistic standards and expectations. While beauty may open doors and confer social advantages, it also imposes a heavy burden of scrutiny and objectification, relegating women to the status of mere commodities valued primarily for their physical appearance. Furthermore, the commodification of beauty intersects with broader issues of power, privilege, and inequality. Women who conform to mainstream beauty ideals are rewarded with validation, attention, and opportunities, while those who deviate from these norms face discrimination, prejudice, and exclusion. The relentless pursuit of beauty and perfection exacts a toll on women's mental and emotional well-being, fueling feelings of inadequacy, insecurity, and self-doubt. The pressure to conform to narrow beauty standards can lead to harmful behaviors such as disordered eating, body dysmorphia, and low self-esteem, perpetuating a cycle of self-destructive patterns and negative self-perceptions.

Aside from their own negative perceptions of themselves, they, too, can possibly view the outside world through a distorted and possibly privileged lens. Men and women will treat them differently, purely because of the biased view they have towards that specific woman's own conventional beauty seen on social media, magazines, etc. Within interpersonal interactions, individuals may be unconsciously influenced by *the halo effect*, a cognitive bias where positive traits, such as physical attractiveness, are associated with other favorable attributes such as intelligence, competence, and likability.[2] This can result in women who conform to beauty standards receiving preferential treatment, validation, and social acceptance, while those who deviate from these norms may face prejudice, discrimination, and marginalization.

This favorability for beautiful women permeates throughout every facet of our lives.[3] Numerous studies have found that hiring managers and recruiters exhibit biases towards candidates perceived as physically attractive.[4],[5],[6] In a competitive job market, attractive individuals are more likely to be selected for interview invitations and job offers compared to equally qualified but less attractive candidates. This bias can be attributed to the halo effect, where positive attributes associated with physical attractiveness (such as confidence, competence, and social skills) influence overall perceptions of the candidate's suitability for the employment role. The influence of physical attractiveness extends to career advancement opportunities, with attractive individuals more likely to be promoted to leadership positions and given greater responsibilities within organizations.[7] This phenomenon, known as the "glass escalator" effect—where men working in traditionally female-dominated professions, such as nursing, teaching, librarianship, and social work, experience structural advantages that enhance their career trajectories—describes the tendency for men and women in traditionally female-dominated fields to experience accelerated career progression and upward mobility due to their perceived fit with leadership stereotypes.

OnlyFans, a subscription-based content platform, has gained notoriety for its promise of financial success and autonomy, particularly for content creators in the adult entertainment industry. With the allure of lucrative earnings and flexible work schedules, OnlyFans has attracted a diverse array of creators, including many Millennial women seeking financial independence and empowerment. But the empowerment narrative surrounding OnlyFans and similar platforms is multifaceted. On the one hand, it offers a platform for sexual expression and autonomy, allowing creators to take ownership of their bodies and how they are represented. On the other, much more eye-opening hand, it perpetuates the commodification of sexuality, raising concerns about the long-term implications for creators' personal and professional lives. The stigma attached to sex work, even in its digital form, can have lasting effects, influencing relationships, mental health, and future employment prospects.

This is nothing new, however; the history of sex work (and its resulting consequences among women) runs deep in American culture. From the days of early European settlement with its lack of women and various compensated relationships, to the so-called "parlor houses" of the 19th century, sex work has been a prominent part of the American story.[8] This expansion was only further catalyzed by the Gold Rush age, where women turned to sex work for financial survival in the developing frontier towns. With the growth of urban areas, red-light districts in cities such as New Orleans' Storyville and San Francisco's Barbary Coast received notoriety not only as places of adult entertainment but of artistic and cultural expression. This time also evidenced a grand-scale mobilization of moral reform that signaled intensification in regulation and criminalization around sex work. The complexities increased during the 20th century when feminist movements questioned traditional perspectives on sex work and raised heated debate about autonomy, exploitation, and defining the boundaries of voluntary sex work and trafficking. That history, with periods of relative tolerance, repression, and activism, is emblematic of a protracted struggle to reconcile societal values with the realities of sex work—a struggle that continues to delineate its legal, social, and economic dimensions in America today.

The rise of OnlyFans also presents a complex moral and ethical dilemma, as creators navigate the blurred boundaries between empowerment, exploitation, and commodification of intimacy. The platform's emphasis on monetizing personal content and cultivating a subscriber base raises questions about the long-term consequences of pursuing quick financial gains at the expense of privacy and dignity. The true dilemma being that when you have a commodity that is so lucrative and so powerful that it could pull you out of poverty and move you into a higher social class (given that you can hide the occupation)—and additionally meet with and socialize with powerful, influential people—it would behoove you to participate, especially with how easily accessible and formulaic it seemingly is. . . . With smartphones becoming more and more advanced, namely in the context of media and camera operation, the phones of would-be OnlyFans content creators are currently powerful enough to start a full production, simply by removing your clothes.

The formula for creating OnlyFans content that is engaging and can gain you copious amounts of revenue goes as follows: (1) You have to have a clear understanding of your audience and what they are looking for. This involves not just showcasing physical beauty but also creating a persona that resonates with subscribers, often through a combination of charm, wit, and the illusion of accessibility and intimacy. (2) Consistency and quality of content are key. Regular updates with high-quality visuals and engaging interactions are essential to retain subscribers and attract new ones. This often means investing in good equipment, learning editing skills, and staying abreast of trends and preferences within the platform. (3) Marketing and self-promotion are critical components. Successful OnlyFans creators are adept at using social media and other digital platforms to promote their content, draw in subscribers from a broader audience, and create a brand around their persona. This requires savvy digital marketing skills and a thick skin to navigate the inevitable scrutiny and backlash. (4) Navigating ethical and personal boundaries is crucial for long-term sustainability. Creators must carefully consider the long-term impacts of their content on their personal lives, relationships, and future career prospects. Setting clear boundaries on what content is shared—and maintaining a level of privacy—is essential to safeguard mental health and personal well-being. (5) Finally, understanding the business side of content creation on OnlyFans is vital. This includes managing finances, understanding the platform's fee structure, and exploring ways to diversify income streams to ensure financial stability beyond the platform. The list goes on and on when it comes to success and how to obtain it on OnlyFans.

While it may not be pleasant to hear, there are two sides to every story, to every coin. OnlyFans, just like any other online adult content website, is a business. Not everyone can be successful, and not everyone has something special. It does require hard work, dedication, a level of persuasion and negotiation skills; thick skin in some instances, and awareness of the world around you and of male psychology. For better or for worse, beautiful women are fully aware of their power in their looks. It's a tale as old as time. The story of empowerment through self-expression and financial independence is predominantly accessible to those who already align with certain acceptable standards of beauty and who can afford the risks associated with being publicly associated with adult content.

This selective empowerment raises questions about the inclusivity and equity of such platforms. It challenges us to consider who is left out of the narrative and why, shedding light on the broader societal structures and biases that continue to govern access to opportunities and platforms for empowerment. . . . But is the so-called "empowerment" real? Could the lives of OnlyFans models (namely the ones doing adult content) be as lavish and as fulfilling as seen through the lens of their curated social media platforms? After all, the grass always seems greener on the other side, as they say. The OnlyFans phenomenon is emblematic of a larger societal trend towards a so-called "gig economy" and precarious labor. Just as ride-sharing apps and freelance marketplaces have transformed traditional employment landscapes, platforms like OnlyFans represent a new frontier in gig work—where the product is, unfortunately, one's own body and persona. For women (and men) that do not mind this objectification, it can indeed be very lucrative . . . but it does come with a hefty cost.

Pornstars, male or female, live very interesting and peculiar lives, indeed. Some positive, some negative. It's easy to see the positive aspects more than ever, due to social media's availability to an influential early-twenty-year-old. But the negative is either easily unseen or just blatantly ignored. Despite the potential for financial success and social mobility, individuals in the adult entertainment industry often face stigmatization, discrimination, and judgment from society at large. This stigma can extend into personal relationships, leading to isolation and strained family connections. Furthermore, the physical and emotional toll of working in adult entertainment can be significant. Performers may face health risks, including physical injury and exposure to sexually transmitted infections. The psychological impact can be equally daunting, with many performers experiencing issues such as depression, anxiety, and substance abuse. The professional life of a pornstar is also fraught with challenges. The industry is highly competitive, and success often depends on maintaining a certain physical appearance and being willing to perform a wide range of acts. The pressure to stay relevant and in demand can lead to a relentless cycle of surgeries, physical enhancements, and pushing personal boundaries. Moreover, the transient nature of success in the adult entertainment industry means that many performers find themselves struggling to maintain a stable income as they age or as industry trends shift.

The monetization of intimacy raises complex questions about the nature of personal connections in the digital age. In a world where affection, attention, and intimacy can be commodified and sold, the lines between genuine personal interactions and transactional relationships become increasingly blurred. This shift has the potential to alter how individuals understand and navigate personal relationships, with far-reaching consequences for concepts of love, friendship, and community. . . . But the real question then becomes: Who are the buyers of said OnlyFans content? Currently, 190 million active users use OnlyFans (and 2.1 million of those are creators),[9] with a user growth rate of 1291.85% between 2019 and 2021. The statistics on gender demographics remain unclear. Some show that 87% of users are male, 10% of users are female, and 3% of users would rather not say their gender. Other statistics claim that a majority of OnlyFans users (60%) are male, leaving the rest female with a very small percentage non-binary.[10] It would be unfair to place complete blame (or stigma) on the women who dominate the creator's market of OnlyFans; the users, the majority of male users namely, who make up most of the viewership, should also be to blame. Those seeking to find an attractive person to chat with and find a supposed "Girlfriend Experience" appear to be in my eyes profoundly lonely, and, perhaps, flawed beyond measure. . . . But that is a conversation to be had elsewhere.

Reader's Group Discussion Questions

- The chapter presents the idea that conventional beauty and genetics afford certain privileges while also perpetuating unrealistic standards. Discuss how this duality affects women's roles in society and their self-perception. Do you think the benefits outweigh the disadvantages?

- The text explores the concept of the "level of attractiveness" and its hypothetical correlation with life success. How do you feel about the implications of measuring someone's value based on their physical appearance? Discuss the ethical considerations and societal impacts of such a practice.

- OnlyFans is portrayed as both empowering and exploitative, especially for women. Discuss the different facets of empowerment and exploitation presented in the chapter. Can OnlyFans truly be a platform for female empowerment, or does it reinforce existing societal inequities?

- The chapter delves into the historical context of sex work and its evolution into digital platforms like OnlyFans. Discuss how the history of sex work has shaped contemporary attitudes and the legal and social frameworks surrounding it.

- The narrative raises questions about the nature of work and labor in the context of the gig economy, comparing traditional jobs to creating content on OnlyFans. Discuss the parallels and differences between these types of work. What are the implications for labor rights and employment structures?

- The phenomenon of OnlyFans and the gig economy leads to a commodification of intimacy and personal relationships. How does this shift impact societal views on love, friendship, and human connection? Discuss the long-term effects this might have on personal and societal levels.

- Finally, the chapter addresses the stigma faced by individuals in the adult entertainment industry and the challenges they endure. Reflect on the societal and personal consequences of this stigma. How can society move towards a more understanding and supportive approach to individuals working in these professions?

Footnotes:

[1] Yamim, A., Nique, W., & Borges, A. (2016). Are We All Equal in the Face of Social Comparison? The Moderating Role of Consumer Values: A Structured Abstract. , 881-886. https://doi.org/10.1007/978-3-319-26647-3_191.

[2] Nisbett, R., & Wilson, T. (1977). The Halo Effect: Evidence for Unconscious Alteration of Judgments.. *Journal of Personality and Social Psychology*, 35, 250-256. https://doi.org/10.1037/0022-3514.35.4.250.

[3] Anderson, C., John, O., Keltner, D., & Kring, A. (2001). Who attains social status? Effects of personality and physical attractiveness in social groups.. Journal of personality and social psychology, 81 1, 116-32 . https://doi.org/10.1037//0022-3514.81.1.116.

[4] Watkins, L., & Johnston, L. (2000). Screening job applicants : The impact of physical attractiveness and application quality. International Journal of Selection and Assessment, 8, 76-84. https://doi.org/10.1111/1468-2389.00135.

[5] Shahani-Denning, C., Andreoli, N., Snyder, J., Tevet, R., & Fox, S. (2011). The Effects of Physical Attractiveness and Gender on Selection Decisions: An Experimental Study. *The International Journal of Management*, 28, 16.

[6] Shahani-Denning, C., Dudhat, P., Tevet, R., & Andreoli, N. (2010). Effect of Physical Attractiveness on Selection Decisions in India and the United States. *The International Journal of Management*, 27, 37.

[7] Morrow, P., McElroy, J., Stamper, B., & Wilson, M. (1990). The Effects of Physical Attractiveness and Other Demographic Characteristics on Promotion Decisions. *Journal of Management*, 16, 723 - 736. https://doi.org/10.1177/014920639001600405.

[8] Ditmore, M. (2010). Prostitution and Sex Work. https://doi.org/10.5860/choice.48-6038.

[9] Daniel, Ch. December 29th, 2023. *SignHouse.* "OnlyFans Users and Revenue Statistics (2024)". https://www.usesignhouse.com/blog/onlyfans-users

[10] Lindner, Jannik. April 24th, 2024. *Gitnux.* "Must-Know Onlyfans Gender Statistics [Latest Report]". https://gitnux.org/onlyfans-gender-statistics/#:~:text=The%20majority%20(60%25)%20of,creators%20self%2Didentify%20as%20LGBTQ.

[the modern millennial male: lack of commitment, the loss of integrity, diminished self-esteem, and a loss of collective masculinity]

Men have undoubtedly kept the motor of the world running. They have built towers, buildings, planes, ships . . . They invented the printing press[1], invented sanitation[2] . . . The modern world would take a huge loss if it weren't for the men who helped foster its inception. We need men . . . a lot. We need them more than we'd all care to admit. We need the builders, the inventors, and the fathers to guide us and center us. These are both fundamental and critical to our humanity's success.

For those that asked themselves the question: "But what about women? After all, they keep the world running too!" To this, I have to say that you are, yes, absolutely correct. Behind every man is a fantastic, supportive woman. But not just in the context of men and women together. Females have empowered us and moved us forward, too. I can go on and on about the successes of women, but for now, we need to highlight the successes of men—and give appreciation for them.

The world almost never gives appreciation for men, purely because we view men as replaceable, expendable, and expect them to have gratitude for having the privilege of servicing our lives. A study found that the dynamics of recognition and praise in dual-earner couples, particularly focusing on how each partner's income and contributions are perceived, uncovers a double standard: women tend to receive more praise than men for their financial contributions.[3] While money is not the end-all, be-all, it does showcase value and support in making lives easier—hallmarks of what we view as *success* in America.

If you would like examples of men being replaceable and expendable, look no further than our military. The military, rooted in history and society's traditional gender roles, highlights men's association with high-risk roles like combat. This concept ties into military masculinity, valorizing physical strength, bravery, and sacrifice.[4] While discussions on gender in the military often focus on women's challenges in a male-dominated sphere, there's also a significant impact on men, framed by expectations of masculinity and their roles as soldiers. The military acts as a sort of *masculinity maker*, reinforcing ideals that include a readiness to undertake dangerous tasks for the greater good. This expectation is part of military socialization, shaping male soldiers' views on their roles and identities,[5] including accepting risk and expendability as part of their duty.

While this approach by the military, in the context of how men are treated, might seem harsh and malevolent, it has paradoxically left many men feeling appreciative and endowed with a significant sense of purpose. Exposure to military stressors like deployment can significantly affect well-being, with longer and first deployments linked to higher distress levels among soldiers, indicating the impact on mental health. However, seeing positive outcomes from military service, such as improved mastery, self-esteem, and coping skills, can enhance psychological resilience in veterans, reducing PTSD symptoms.[6],[7] This highlights the importance of acknowledging the dual effects of military service on mental health.

It appears that we all (including men, paradoxically) need men, and men acutely need us. We are all drawn to a collective connection and togetherness that appears lost in our modern world. . . . With higher depression rates, higher anxiety, and an overall lower testosterone level among Millennials and Gen-Zers,[8] it is no wonder that there are higher self-esteem issues between these two generations. . . . Well, not always higher . . . In an article by the *Times* entitled "Millennials: The Me Me Me Generation," there is a quote that showcases that Millennials have a sort of split personality when it comes to self-esteem, both having great initial (or first-impression) self-confidence, but falling short when it comes to maintaining their self-confidence: "It turns out that self-esteem is great for getting a job or hooking up at a bar but not so great for keeping a job or a relationship."[9]

It's hard not to blame social media for both inflating and deflating the self-confidence/self-esteem of Millennials and Gen-Zers. But it's also hard not to blame society in general for the discrepancy, too. Our media, our Hollywood movies, our schools, and our culture leaves men falling at the wayside and promotes women's empowerment as the highest ideal. While women's empowerment and overall self-esteem is important to our society, there is a fine line (and balance) when it comes to eliminating a whole generation of men from your life and deeming them not useful to your life.

The "Red Pill" concept has become a pivotal part of modern discourse surrounding gender relations, emanating largely from online communities and gaining traction for its controversial views on masculinity, feminism, and societal roles. The term itself is borrowed from the science fiction film *The Matrix*, where taking the "red pill" means embracing the harsh truth of reality over the blissful ignorance of illusion, presented as a choice between a red pill and a blue pill. . . . In the context of gender discussions, the Red Pill ideology is built around the belief that men have been misled—by feminism, by political correctness, and by societal shifts—into denying their true nature and the realities of what it means to be a man. Proponents argue that conventional dating advice, gender roles, and expectations have been constructed not to benefit men but to placate and advance feminist agendas. The Red Pill philosophy, in response, encourages men to awaken to these "truths" and to reject the societal norms that they believe emasculate them.

According to classic Red Pill thinking, men need to *wake up* and see things for how they really are. At the heart of this is the belief in clear biological differences between men and women that dictate their roles and behaviors. Red Pillers argue that these traditional roles are not just natural but also good for both men and women, making everyone happier and more fulfilled. They see modern challenges to these roles as the root of a lot of today's unhappiness and confusion. When it comes to dating and relationships between men and women, the Red Pill crowd is all about men being bold, assertive, and in charge —qualities they think have been lost but are naturally attractive to women. They're also pretty skeptical about marriage and long-term relationships these days, arguing that the legal and cultural climate is stacked against men, especially if things go south.

The Red Pill world comes with its own lingo too. You'll hear terms like "Alpha" for dominant guys, "Beta" for the more submissive ones, and "AWALT" (*all women are like that*), a catch-all phrase they use to describe behaviors in women they view as malicious or manipulative. But it's not just about dating. This philosophy spills over into broader issues like men's rights, the impact of feminism on society, and how men are valued in today's world.

There's a lot of talk about the decline of traditional masculinity and what it means to be a man today. Some of the talk views the whole of masculinity as dangerous to society. Amongst feminists, there is a term for it, too. It is called "Toxic Masculinity." This phrase, too, appears to be a catch-all, in regards to feminist women labeling men as *too masculine*.

Critics of Red Pill ideology have slammed it for promoting negative views of women and misunderstanding what feminism really is about. They argue that, while it's crucial to talk about the challenges men face, the often aggressive and bitter tone of Red Piller's discussions might do more harm than good, entrenching unhealthy attitudes toward women and relationships. . . . So, the Red Pill is like a tough-love take on modern gender issues. It's controversial, no doubt, and whether you see it as a much-needed wake-up call or a problematic ideology, it is definitely sparking a lot of conversations about the state of men and women today.

Despite a culture change, the battle of the sexes, it appears, is still in full swing, but in a vastly different context. . . .

But what exactly is the term "Toxic Masculinity"? Through a feminist lens, Toxic masculinity refers to a set of behaviors and beliefs that dictate how men are socially expected to conduct themselves based on an aggressive, rigid gender norm. These societal expectations often glorify stoicism, strength, virility, dominance, and control, while suppressing traits such as emotional vulnerability, expressivity, and nurturing. The concept is crucial for understanding certain problematic behaviors that are traditionally accepted as masculine and often contribute to detrimental social and psychological outcomes.

Despite what a Red Piller might think, the term "toxic masculinity" through the lens of a *real feminist* (and not one of the New Age persuasion) does not imply that masculinity itself is inherently toxic. Instead, it highlights aspects of prescribed masculine norms that can lead to harm against oneself and others. These harmful traits are perpetuated by cultural narratives and social structures that reinforce traditional gender roles. For instance, boys might grow up hearing "men don't cry" or "show them who's boss," phrases that encourage emotional suppression and aggressive behavior. Traits that may have left weaker and more sensitive men down a path of destruction or depression.

The narrative that Millennial men lack commitment, according to some varieties of publications like The Guardian[10], Cosmopolitan[11], and Medium[12], whether in relationships, careers, or life goals, is often plainly heard and is a sentiment that appears widely agreed upon. Yet, this lack of commitment that these men harbor might actually be understood as a rational response to a society that no longer upholds the values of loyalty and reliability that once guided men. As societal expectations shift and the rewards for steadfast commitment dwindle, men's reluctance to engage deeply in such spheres becomes more understandable. This isn't a failure of individual men but a reflection of a broader cultural transformation.

Integrity, a cornerstone of traditional masculine virtue, appears to be in decline. However, this loss is not self-generated but is influenced by external criticisms of what it means to be a man today. Constant messages suggesting that traditional male behaviors are inherently toxic or problematic erode this core value. When the natural traits of men are portrayed negatively, it challenges their ability to maintain a clear sense of moral and personal integrity. On top of that, diminished self-esteem among men is a growing concern, as I have said. From a young age, men receive mixed signals that praise vulnerability while simultaneously condemning the traditional male expressions of strength and leadership. This conflicting messaging can confuse and demoralize, leading to an erosion of self-esteem.

The concept of collective masculinity, or a shared understanding of what it means to be a man, is also fading. This decline is partly due to the disappearance of traditional spaces where men learned about leadership, accountability, and resilience—qualities essential for personal development. Concepts that, ironically, can really only be taught by our fathers. 43% of U.S. children live without their father.[13] This means that it affects our daughters, too. As these communal experiences vanish, replaced by isolated and often virtual interactions, the guideposts that once helped young men navigate their journey to mature masculinity are no longer as visible or as valued. . . .

Addressing these challenges requires a cultural reevaluation that re-embraces the positive aspects of masculinity. This includes fostering environments that celebrate and cultivate masculine virtues, advocating for strong role models who exemplify these traits, and encouraging a societal acknowledgment of the unique contributions men make. By restoring these values, society can help men regain a sense of purpose and identity, leading to healthier outcomes for individuals and communities alike. . . . This perspective is not about clinging to outdated norms but rather recognizing the importance of balance and respect for the intrinsic qualities that have traditionally been admired in men. By reaffirming these virtues, we can better support men in fulfilling their potential and contributing positively to society.

As we have seen, traditional roles have evolved, and with this evolution comes a redefinition of what it means to be a man in today's world. This redefinition is often riddled with contradictions. On one hand, the persistent push for rugged individualism and self-reliance remains strong; on the other, there's an increasing acknowledgment of the importance of vulnerability and emotional openness in men. This shift, while positive, is not without its challenges. Men are often caught in a tug-of-war between embracing a new, more emotionally open persona and adhering to the stoic, reserved image that has traditionally defined masculinity.

This dichotomy is particularly evident in the workplace. In industries traditionally dominated by men, such as technology and engineering, there's a growing pressure to adapt to new norms that value diversity and emotional intelligence over the old command-and-control leadership styles.[14] However, the transition is not smooth. Many men struggle with this shift, feeling an erosion of their traditional roles without clear guidance on how to enact their identities within this new framework. This often leads to a sense of displacement and a search for identity, which can exacerbate feelings of depression and anxiety.

The influence of social media adds another layer of complexity. Platforms that often promote unattainable lifestyles or body images can lead to feelings of inadequacy and failure. The constant comparison to others' curated lives can make it difficult for individuals to appreciate their own successes and foster genuine self-esteem. Furthermore, the culture of instant feedback on social media can create a scenario where external validation becomes the primary source of self-worth, which is both fleeting and shallow.

To address these issues, it's essential to foster environments where men can explore their identities without judgment. Educational programs that focus on emotional intelligence, resilience, and mental health can equip men with the tools necessary to navigate the complexities of modern societal expectations. Additionally, creating spaces in both professional and personal settings that encourage open dialogue about masculinity and mental health can help break down the stigmas that often prevent men from seeking help. . . .

Expanding on the theme of creating supportive environments for men, it's crucial to cultivate settings that allow men to express and explore their identities in a more comprehensive and healthy manner. Educational programs that emphasize emotional intelligence, resilience, and mental health are fundamental. By integrating these topics into school curriculums, workplace training, and community workshops, men can gain the necessary tools to navigate the complexities of contemporary societal expectations. This education should start early, embedding emotional awareness and mental health literacy into the fabric of lifelong learning, ensuring men are equipped to handle life's challenges from a young age. . . . For our youth, our boys, are going to define the men in the future.

Reader's Group Discussion Questions

- The chapter begins by highlighting the significant contributions of men throughout history. Discuss how these contributions have shaped modern society. Do you think these achievements are often overlooked in contemporary discussions about gender roles?

- The chapter touches on how men and women are differently recognized for their contributions, especially in dual-earner households. Why do you think this double standard exists? How can society work towards more equitable recognition of contributions regardless of gender?

- The role of the military in reinforcing traditional masculine ideals is discussed extensively. How do you think this impacts the identity and mental health of men in the military? What changes, if any, would you propose to the way masculinity is framed within military culture?

- The chapter suggests that social media has a significant impact on the self-esteem of Millennials and Gen-Zers. What are some of the positive and negative effects of social media on young men's self-esteem? How can individuals and communities mitigate the negative impacts?

- Considering the pressures and contradictions mentioned regarding modern masculinity, what are some of the biggest challenges facing young men today? How can these challenges be addressed by communities and policymakers?

- The text discusses the evolving role of men in society and the need for a cultural reevaluation that embraces positive aspects of masculinity. What would this reevaluation look like in practical terms? How can men balance traditional masculine virtues with the need for emotional openness and vulnerability?

Footnotes:

---

[1] Dittmar, J. (2011). Information Technology and Economic Change: The Impact of The Printing Press. Quarterly Journal of Economics, 126, 1133-1172. https://doi.org/10.1093/QJE/QJR035.

[2] Yannopoulos, S., Yapijakis, C., Kaiafa-Saropoulou, A., Antoniou, G., & Angelakis, A. (2017). History of sanitation and hygiene technologies in the Hellenic world. Journal of Water Sanitation and Hygiene for Development, 7, 163-180. https://doi.org/10.2166/WASHDEV.2017.178.

[3] Deutsch, F., Roksa, J., & Meeske, C. (2003). How Gender Counts When Couples Count Their Money. Sex Roles, 48, 291-304. https://doi.org/10.1023/A:1022982328840.

[4] Mankayi, N. (2011). MALE CONSTRUCTIONS AND RESISTANCE TO WOMEN IN THE MILITARY. Scientia Militaria: South African Journal of Military Studies, 34, 44-64. https://doi.org/10.5787/34-2-23.

[5] Arkin, W., & Dobrofsky, L. (1978). Military Socialization and Masculinity. Journal of Social Issues, 34, 151-168. https://doi.org/10.1111/J.1540-4560.1978.TB02546.X.

[6] Adler, A., Huffman, A., Bliese, P., & Castro, C. (2005). The impact of deployment length and experience on the well-being of male and female soldiers.. Journal of occupational health psychology, 10 2, 121-37 . https://doi.org/10.1037/1076-8998.10.2.121.

[7] Aldwin, C., Levenson, M., & Spiro, A. (1994). Vulnerability and resilience to combat exposure: can stress have lifelong effects?. Psychology and aging, 9 1, 34-44 . https://doi.org/10.1037//0882-7974.9.1.34.

[8] Dr Joshua Smith, Research Scientist, MBBS, BMedSci, PGCertMedEd. January 10th, 2024. "Why do Gen Z and millennial men have lower testosterone levels?" Medichecks. https://www.medichecks.com/blogs/testosterone/why-do-gen-z-and-millennial-men-have-lower-testosterone#:~:text=It's%20normal%20for%20testosterone%20levels,levels%20compared%20to%20their%20predecessors.

[9] Time Staff. May 20th, 2013. *TIME Magazine.* "Millennials: The Me Me Me Generation". https://time.com/247/millennials-the-me-me-me-generation/

[10] Mahdawi, Arwa. February 25th, 2023. *The Guardian.* "Why have young men fallen out of love with romantic relationships?". https://www.theguardian.com/commentisfree/2023/feb/25/young-men-relationships-study-week-in-patriarchy

[11] Peyser, Eve. July 15th, 2016. *Cosmopolitan.* "Men Who Are Afraid of Commitment Explain Why". https://www.cosmopolitan.com/sex-love/a61262/why-dont-men-commit/

[12] Dr. Paras. August 23rd, 2020. Medium. "Fear of Commitment — Millennial's Biggest Struggle in Relationship". https://drparas.medium.com/fear-of-commitment-millennials-biggest-struggle-in-relationship-1e24f98e8a40

[13] Lindner, Jannik. December 20th, 2023. Gitnux. "Must-Know Fatherless Homes Statistics [Latest Report]". https://gitnux.org/fatherless-homes-statistics/#:~:text=Highlights%3A%20Fatherless%20Homes%20Statistics,anger%20come%20from%20fatherless%20homes.

[14] Lappalainen, P. (2020). Educating for Diversity Management in Engineering. 2020 IEEE Global Engineering Education Conference (EDUCON), 1483-1486. https://doi.org/10.1109/EDUCON45650.2020.9125329.

[the marriage shortfall: mass disinterest in commitment and group indifference towards the nuclear family]

Young people of every generation—and in all cultural backgrounds—have struggled with the concept of marriage. As an institution, it has been an essential part of human society serving several needs: legal, social, and economic.[1],[2] Its history tells us about the changing dynamics of human relations, societal norms, and cultural values, which changed over time and geography. The history of marriage began in prehistoric times. Mostly, early marriages were arranged due to strategic alliances, wealth consolidation, or population growth. Marriages in the past were more for property and alliances rather than for love.[3]

It shouldn't be surprising that marriage rates are decreasing in general among not just Millennials but among nearly every generation. Since the 1970s, marriage patterns have evolved significantly, with a notable increase in the age at first marriage. This shift has contributed to an overall decline in marriage rates.[4]

In ancient civilizations like Egypt, Greece, and Rome, people often married young and to maintain power. In Rome, for example, the head of the family arranged many marriages, highlighting that marriage was a crucial part of family and societal structure. During the Renaissance, the idea of marriage began to shift towards individual choice and love. However, even then, marriages were still heavily influenced by economic, social, and political factors. Major changes came in the 19th and 20th centuries: The concept of marrying for love became more widely accepted, and women's rights within marriage gained recognition—and eventually, same-sex marriages started being legally recognized in many countries. . . .

What exactly is influencing a decrease in Millennial marriage rates? To put this into perspective, only 13% of women born in the 1990s were married by age 22, compared to a staggering 69% of women born in the 1940s. Looking ahead, it's projected that between 68% and 72% of Millennials will be married by age 40, which is lower than any other generation of Americans before them.[5] This shift reflects broader changes in societal norms and economic pressures that influence Millennials' life choices.

Cohabitation, or living together without being married, offers a practical alternative to marriage. It allows couples to share living expenses and build a life together without the formalities and potential legal complications of marriage. As marriage rates decline, cohabitation rates have risen significantly among Millennials.[6] Over 8 million Millennial couples in the U.S. are cohabitating instead of marrying.[7] Traditionally, marriage was viewed as a cornerstone of adult life, crucial for personal stability and happiness. Millennials, however, are redefining these norms. Many see marriage as one of several pathways to a fulfilling life, rather than a necessary milestone.[8] This change is partly due to a stronger emphasis on individual goals and career development. Millennials often prioritize their careers and personal growth, seeing these as foundational to their overall well-being.

Economic factors also play a significant role in Millennials' attitudes toward marriage. Student loan debt and economic insecurity are substantial barriers.[9] The average Millennial carries a considerable amount of student loan debt, which can delay or deter marriage. Financial stability is a common prerequisite for marriage among young adults, and high debt levels can hinder the ability to achieve this stability. Economic insecurity, characterized by stagnant wages and a precarious job market, further complicates matters. Millennials often face uncertainty in their careers, making it difficult to commit to the financial responsibilities that marriage entails. The pressure to be financially stable before marrying is higher than ever, pushing many Millennials to postpone marriage or avoid it altogether.

The value and institution of marriage require that the two individuals in question be more able and willing to collaborate cohesively. In our digital age, when problems or issues arise in Millennial (or Gen-Z) relationships, it is easier than ever to withdraw from those relationships and surf social media, contributing to a lack of communication when it most counts. The key to nearly every successful relationship would have to be two things: (1) Both parties have to be willing to not leave under any *reasonable* circumstance, through the bad and the good (unless there is an outright safety concern, or if they purely do not mesh well with your values), and (2) The parties have to have honest communication on nearly everything in order to build a true sense of trust and further grant mutual understanding of each other's values, needs, wants, and desires. If all goes well, both parties will fulfill what they respectively require—the majority of the time, we all hope. . . .

The point is that people make mistakes, and both parties individually have to know that and understand that there are going to be faults in the other person. If the person struggles with a problem, discloses it to you ahead of time, and you both work through it together, then that will create *love* and *trust*—especially if they both come out of it successfully beating said problem. Research indicates that sharing personal struggles and working through them together can strengthen trust and intimacy in a relationship. Self-disclosure is crucial for building emotional closeness.[10] This seems both harder and easier than ever with the rise of the internet. It would appear that communication access is simple, but the bevy of options and unrealistic examples and expectations of relationships run rampant. An example would be social media personalities curating their perfect lives, perfect bodies, and perfect lifestyles. Perfect everything. When your feed is bombarded with the highest ideal at all times, what is forgotten is that life is often ugly and not what you'd expect: sometimes in either a good or bad way.

For women, a social media feed showcasing the highest ideal might feature attractive, wealthy men with lavish lifestyles. While this is appealing, it is worth considering that life might be better with a more simplistic approach—a blue-collar man who adores and cares for you, showering you with love and affection. For men, the highest ideal might be a Victoria's Secret supermodel with a cute smile, agreeable nature, and a constant enthusiasm for sex. An average male's feed is often filled with such grotesque imagery, sometimes linked to the woman's OnlyFans account via a convenient link in bio. This creates a fantasy, warping the definition of what a woman is. In reality, men should seek out real women who love them genuinely and are committed to making them happy, relaxed, and content. Looks and persona aren't everything, and this understanding is most crucial.

Meeting and keeping a man or woman is a daunting and difficult task that not everyone wants to commit to. Laborious in the same way your job is; it does not always have good days just the same. The defining moments of marriage are not how you handle the good times but how you handle and fight through the bad times—this is a distinction that our youth may be missing. . . .

The upward trend of dating app usage looms over the populace. Currently, 30% of U.S. adults use these platforms, with a significant 53% of users aged 18 to 29, and 37% aged 30 to 49.[11] This shift highlights a stark difference in dating dynamics between pre-internet and post-internet generations—and with this difference, a change in how relationships and marriage are both viewed and choreographed.

Constant swiping, short blurbs, and curated headshots of prospective boyfriends or girlfriends can never beat real, face-to-face meet-ups in a common-interest location where small-talk, laughs, and connection flourish. That's what is missing with new generations. When the division between romance is quite literally our screens, it makes viewing someone as a real, live person with thoughts and feelings more easily disregarded. . . . Furthermore, the fast-paced, disposable nature of modern dating apps contributes to a decline in commitment. The ease of swiping right on potential matches creates a paradox of choice, where the abundance of options makes it difficult to settle on one person. This phenomenon, known as the "paradox of choice,"[12] can lead to decision fatigue and a reluctance to commit, as users are always left wondering if there might be someone better just a swipe away.

Our peers aren't much help, either. When someone faces issues with their partner that could be resolved through traditional communication and mutual affection, seeing the seemingly "perfect" lives of others on social media can make the idea of finding a new partner more appealing than working through relationship challenges. Excessive social media use can decrease relationship satisfaction, increase conflicts, and lead to social media addiction, further worsening relationship problems.[13] Additionally, the rise of "hookup culture" among Millennials has shifted the focus from long-term relationships to casual encounters. This cultural shift, fueled by dating apps and social media, has normalized short-term, non-committal interactions over the pursuit of meaningful, long-term partnerships. While this approach to relationships can offer freedom and exploration, it can also result in a lack of deep emotional connections and a greater sense of loneliness.

Media representation of marriage tends to favor unmarried couples over those traditionally married. In the top 25 most popular films of the '90s (the formidable years of Millennials), married partners were underrepresented in sexual behaviors compared to their unmarried counterparts. An analysis of these films revealed that married couples accounted for only 15% of depicted sexual behavior, which was mostly limited to passionate kissing. In contrast, unmarried couples were more frequently shown engaging in implied intercourse.[14] Moreover, racial minorities were also underrepresented in television, particularly in the context of interracial relationships. Black and Asian pairings were seldom depicted in prime-time television dramas. When these relationships did appear, they often encountered narrative challenges that reinforced racial hierarchies, and few achieved stable romantic outcomes such as marriage.[15]

For individuals looking to "start over" and marry someone they adore after a previous unsuccessful marriage, the portrayal of stepfamilies in films is often negative or mixed. Some common themes include conflicts with former partners and strained step-parent/child relationships.[16] These portrayals can influence societal views and shape the expectations of stepfamily dynamics, potentially stigmatizing them for impressionable young viewers; viewers that, mind you, could have already been exposed and witnessed their own issues within step-parent dynamics, further solidifying an ingrained belief (i.e., possibly Millennials or Gen-Zers). Such ingrained beliefs can influence young people's outlook on marriage, leading them to view it as less than ideal as they transition into adulthood.

Young adults frequently form attachments to celebrities, which can significantly impact their sense of identity and self-worth. The conduct of celebrities in their relationships often shapes young people's views on their own relationships and identities.[17] Millennials and Gen-Z are particularly susceptible to parasocial relationships, where they develop one-sided connections with celebrities. This phenomenon can skew their perceptions of what constitutes a "normal" or "ideal" relationship, leading them to compare their relationships to the seemingly perfect ones portrayed by celebrities.[18]

It's not just Millennials and Gen-Z who are finding marriage less appealing; our government's policies are also playing a big part. Many government assistance programs, like Temporary Assistance for Needy Families (TANF), reduce benefits for married couples. This means low-income individuals often find it financially smarter to stay single, especially during tough times.[19] It makes it very hard to get ahead, especially through times of hardship. Those who become financially distraught will do anything to survive, including participating in the postponement of would-be marriage.

The tax system seemingly adds to the problem by imposing marriage penalties: Dual-income couples end up paying more taxes than if they were single, which discourages marriage among working-class and middle-income couples. Congress, for example, in the 2005 Deficit Reduction Act, quietly reinstated a marriage penalty by sanctioning states that didn't meet a 35-hour weekly work requirement for 90% of two-parent families, compared to a more lenient 50% work rate for other families.[20] When our government seems to be undermining marriage, it sends a conflicting message to society. These counterproductive policies discourage the very institution that has traditionally supported societal stability and economic growth. Marriage has long been a cornerstone for financial and emotional support, creating environments where children can thrive. Penalizing or disincentivizing marriage doesn't just impact couples—it has broader consequences for family structures and community cohesion.

The combination of financial penalties and reduced benefits for married couples contributes to declining marriage rates, especially among Millennials and Gen-Z. These generations are already facing significant economic challenges like student loan debt, high housing costs, and a volatile job market. Consequently, they are delaying or forgoing marriage altogether, partly due to the financial burdens exacerbated by some of these types of policies. . . .

As marriage rates decline, the demand for alternative forms of social support increases. To foster healthier, more stable communities, we need to reconsider how marriage is treated within our policy frameworks. Encouraging marriage through supportive, rather than punitive measures, could lead to stronger family units and more resilient societies. Policymakers must recognize the complex nature of marriage and work towards creating an environment where marriage is a viable and attractive option for everyone, regardless of economic standing.

Though it is a shame that both Millennials and Gen-Zers are getting married at lower rates, the silver lining lies in their focus on personal growth and career development before committing to marriage. This shift allows for the possibility of more mature and stable relationships when they *do* choose to marry. If you think about it, is marriage truly conducive if you lack a stable future, a positive outlook on that future, and security in managing the responsibilities and uncertainties that come with maintaining a marriage?

Previous generations may have married more often than Millennials and Gen-Zers, but they also experienced a booming economy, significant buying power, and an expectation of continued financial stability. These factors empowered individuals to marry with confidence, especially in an era free from the distractions of online and social media influences. For Millennials and Gen-Zers, it ultimately comes down to a matter of confidence in what the future holds for their generation. Without a stable and secure outlook, it simply is not wise to partake in marriage without ensuring a solid foundation for the future.

Reader's Group Discussion Questions

- How have the historical roles and perceptions of marriage, from ancient civilizations to the Renaissance, influenced modern attitudes toward marriage? What are the key differences in the purpose and structure of marriage in these different eras?

- In what ways do current economic pressures, such as student loan debt and economic insecurity, affect Millennials' and Gen-Z's attitudes towards marriage? How do you think these financial burdens compare to those faced by previous generations?

- What are the advantages and disadvantages of cohabitation as an alternative to marriage for Millennials and Gen-Z? Do you think the rise in cohabitation reflects a permanent shift in relationship norms, or is it a response to current economic conditions?

- How has the rise of social media and dating apps changed the dynamics of forming and maintaining romantic relationships? Discuss the "paradox of choice" in the context of modern dating and its impact on commitment and relationship satisfaction.

- How do government policies, such as tax penalties and reduced benefits for married couples, discourage marriage? What changes in policy do you think could encourage more people to consider marriage as a viable and attractive option?

Footnotes:

[1] Bethmann, D., & Kvasnička, M. (2011). The institution of marriage. *Journal of Population Economics*, 24, 1005-1032. https://doi.org/10.1007/S00148-010-0312-1.

[2] Becker, G. (1973). A Theory of Marriage: Part I. *Journal of Political Economy*, 81, 813 - 846. https://doi.org/10.1086/260084.

[3] Walker, R., Hill, K., Flinn, M., & Ellsworth, R. (2011). Evolutionary History of Hunter-Gatherer Marriage Practices. *PLoS ONE*, 6. https://doi.org/10.1371/journal.pone.0019066.

[4] Rodgers, W., & Thornton, A. (1985). Changing patterns of first marriage in the United States. Demography, 22, 265-279. https://doi.org/10.2307/2061181.

[5] Downey, A. (2015). Will Millennials Ever Get Married?. , 1-5. https://doi.org/10.25080/MAJORA-7B98E3ED-000.

[6] Eickmeyer, K., & Manning, W. (2018). Serial Cohabitation in Young Adulthood: Baby Boomers to Millennials.. Journal of marriage and the family, 80 4, 826-840 . https://doi.org/10.1111/JOMF.12495.

[7] Donevan, Connor. November 1st, 2014. *NPR*. "Millennials Navigate The Ups And Downs Of Cohabitation". https://www.npr.org/2014/11/01/358876955/millennials-navigate-the-ups-and-downs-of-cohabitation

[8] Emelyanova, T., & Shmidt, D. (2019). ROMANTIC RELATIONS AND MARRIAGE IN SOCIAL REPRESENTATIONS OF MILLENNIALS AND BABY-BOOMERS. Bulletin of the Moscow State Regional University (Psychology). https://doi.org/10.18384/2310-7235-2019-1-29-43.

[9] Haneman, V. (2017). Marriage, Millennials, and Massive Student Loan Debt. ERN: Other Macroeconomics: Consumption.

[10] Laurenceau, J.-P., Barrett, L. F., & Pietromonaco, P. R. (1998). Intimacy as an interpersonal process: The importance of self-disclosure, partner disclosure, and perceived partner responsiveness in interpersonal exchanges. Journal of Personality and Social Psychology, 74(5), 1238–1251. https://doi.org/10.1037/0022-3514.74.5.1238

[11] Vogels, Emily A.; McClain, Colleen. February 2nd, 2023. *Pew Research Center*. "Key findings about online dating in the U.S.". https://pewrsr.ch/3HulOib

12 Bersh, Larissa. February 26th, 2020. *The Stanford Daily*. "On the paradox of choice, Tinder". https://stanforddaily.com/2020/02/26/on-the-paradox-of-choice-tinder/

[13] Yahiiaiev, I., Savych, M., & Keller, V. (2020). The Connection between Social Media Use and Relationship Satisfaction. Bulletin of Taras Shevchenko National University of Kyiv. Series "Psychology". https://doi.org/10.17721/bsp.2020.2(12).20.

[14] Dempsey, J., & Reichert, T. (2000). PORTRAYAL OF MARRIED SEX IN THE MOVIES. Sexuality and Culture, 4, 21-36. https://doi.org/10.1007/S12119-000-1019-3.

[15] Washington, M. (2012). Interracial Intimacy: Hegemonic Construction of Asian American and Black Relationships on TV Medical Dramas. Howard Journal of Communications, 23, 253 - 271. https://doi.org/10.1080/10646175.2012.695637.

[16] Leon, K., & Angst, E. (2005). Portrayals of Stepfamilies in Film: Using Media Images in Remarriage Education. Family Relations, 54, 3-23. https://doi.org/10.1111/J.0197-6664.2005.00002.X.

[17] Boon, S., & Lomore, C. (2001). Admirer-celebrity relationships among young adults : Explaining perceptions of celebrity influence on identity. Human Communication Research, 27, 432-465. https://doi.org/10.1111/J.1468-2958.2001.TB00788.X.

[18] Copeland, L., & Lyu, J. (2020). Millennial Consumer's on Instagram: Implications for Luxury Brands vs. Celebrity Influencers: An Abstract. , 97-98. https://doi.org/10.1007/978-3-030-42545-6_19.

[19] Cherlin, A. (2003). Should the Government Promote Marriage?. Contexts, 2, 22 - 29. https://doi.org/10.1525/ctx.2003.2.4.22.

[20] Nice, J. (2007). Promoting Marriage Experimentation: A Class Act?. Washington University Journal of Law and Policy, 24, 31-45.

["our American hate": a country filled with rage, anger, desperation, division, and a lack of compassion?]

America has a long history of hate, a sentiment not unique to this country but prevalent worldwide. Hate is not merely historical; hate is an emotional symptom of current negative affairs in history and society at large. Nobody hates for no reason. There almost always has to be a reason backing it, even if it is simply jealousy. Hate works in the same way that a virus does, silently infiltrating communities and spreading from one individual to another, often mutating and becoming more complex as it embeds itself deeply within the social fabric. But the root cause almost always is backed by the individual's own perceived reason, true or not.

Our country, as of right now in the mid-2020s, is in a very obnoxiously hateful time. Left versus Right. Democrat versus Republican. Arguments and rage are seemingly always looming over our shoulders, at least if you were to surf the media daily—and that includes social media. The power of Cancel Culture continues to wield its force across various sectors, often sparking significant backlash and further dividing communities. This cultural phenomenon, characterized by public shaming and boycotting of individuals and organizations for perceived offenses, has arguably exacerbated the climate of hate. It thrives on the dichotomy of 'us versus them,' which has deep roots in American society, often reflecting larger socio-political divisions.

Economic insecurity and class resentment significantly contribute to societal hate. Individuals or groups who feel economically disenfranchised may direct their frustrations toward other communities, blaming them for their hardships. This sentiment is often fueled by populist rhetoric that paints certain groups as the 'other,' responsible for economic troubles, whether they be immigrants, racial minorities, or political adversaries.[1] Meanwhile, the stark political polarization seen in recent years is not just a matter of differing opinions but has evolved into deeply ingrained identity politics. Each side views the other not merely as opponents but as enemies, with media and political leaders often amplifying these divisions for their own gain. Such an environment fosters hate by demonizing the opposing side, making compromise and dialogue increasingly difficult.

The easiest and most blatant example of how hate can fester and intensify, especially through social media, mainstream media, and Hollywood media, would have to be the summer of 2020. Coined ironically by some as the "2020 Summer of Love,"[2] this particular time in our country was most disturbing and telling of present America. Arguably the most important and historic election of our modern times, both presidents seemingly hell-bend on who has the most extreme rhetoric to espouse that their respective parties favor the most. The then-candidate Joe Biden called the Black Lives Matter (BLM) riots during that time a "historic movement for justice,"[3] despite the riots causing between 1-2 billion dollars worth of property damages,[4] including black-owned property.

What truly exacerbated the riots was the George Floyd tragedy where an officer kneeled on his neck for 9-minutes and 29-seconds,[5] and it was all caught on camera for everyone to spectate. Americans—and the rest of the world—were on lockdown and sheltered. The riots themselves did not cause the lockdown—it was because there was a global pandemic, due to the COVID-19 virus. The stagnancy of everyone being cooped up inside, and social media broadcasting such a horrific event, made everyone involved in the BLM riots band together on social media and wreak havoc all across the United States. By early June, protests were so widespread that over 200 American cities had imposed curfews and half of the United States had activated the National Guard. Derek Chauvin, who had already faced at least 17 other misconduct complaints before the incident with Floyd, was arrested on May 29th, 2020. He was charged with second-degree murder, third-degree murder, and second-degree manslaughter.

While Biden may have taken a hard stance in favor of the BLM riots, despite how divisive and tragic they may have been, then-president Donald Trump did not do better. During the presidential debates, the moderator (and Biden, indirectly) asked if Trump would outright condemn right-wing militia groups like The Proud Boys. Trump failed to condemn them. Instead, he said, "Proud Boys, stand back and stand by."[6] Following the president's remarks, leaders and supporters of the Proud Boys celebrated on social media. A Telegram channel, an instant messaging service used by the group, which boasted over 5,000 members, displayed the phrases "Stand Back" and "Stand By" prominently above and below the group's logo.[7] Biden was quick to post an ad on his Twitter profile showcasing and painting Trump to be in support of the right-wing militia group.[8] That election felt like a bloodbath. And arguably it *was* with how many people got hurt or even died that year.

The election of 2020 concluded with Donald Trump's loss, due to the copious amounts of mail-in ballads that came in in the dead of night that favored Biden. Other alleged shenanigans were present, and Donald Trump touted election fraud. With this rhetoric in full swing, these extreme right-wing militia groups, aside from The Proud Boys, protested in front of the Capital on January 6th, 2021, the day the votes for Biden's victory were finalized. The protest turned into a riot, then an outright storming of the United States Capital, doing 30-million dollars worth of damage, according to *The New York Times*.[9] If you were to take the damages numbers in comparison, the BLM riots did approximately between 33-66 times the amount that the January 6th riots did. Despite the damages discrepancy, it was widely said through many Twitter feeds that the Capital being stormed was worse, mostly because it was a government building and not private property. At that point, it both revealed and appeared to me, personally, through viewing through a center lens, that the Left valued government property (Socialism/Communism) over private property, and the Right valued private property (Capitalism) over government property. Both of these were on brand with their parties. . . .

All of this is to simply illustrate that even through all of this division, the only beacon of hope left was the office of the United States president. Even still, the two candidates who were running against one another were as extremely divided as could be. It was a reflection of the state of the country. For anyone who looks towards our representatives in government as a means to lead the country's fate, including the social state of the country, both these two candidates appeared to be lacking in that department. The hate and division in this country is so great and so powerful and so divided, that it makes total and complete sense that generations like Boomers, Gen-X, Millennials, Gen-Z, and even the Alphas, appear to be grossly at odds. A country has to stay together, regardless of political affiliations, creed, race, or anything else. . . . It is sad to say, but communication technology and its easy accessibility are both our gifts and our curses as a society, especially in the year 2020. Sometimes knowing about too much negative information can turn you crazy. . . .

O ur social media appears to be powered by AI. The one goal of social media companies is—and always has been—engagement. The easiest and most effective form of engagement is shock or outrage. Social media companies created algorithms that will purposely turn a user into a media junkie for all things negative. They do this to gain more revenue, produce more ads, and keep you on the app as long as possible. Hate is the one thing this style of formula brings about. If you come across something online that personally offends you or gets under your skin, there is a good chance that AI and its algorithms have curated the viewership of that content for you. These social media companies are evil in that aspect. It's a weaponization of our emotions; hate and outrage being the bread and butter that they strive for. A social media junkie who spends all day on their site with the intent of looking up negativity, things that bother them, shock them, scare them, or outright make themselves hateful towards any one thing . . . well, my friends, that is a top-tier user in the eyes of these social media companies. The reason is because they can easily entice that person to open the application on their phone, and *keep* them there on the app—using almost little to no effort or resources. . . .

Hate and resentment that fester in this way can create an *echo chamber effect*, where users are shown content that aligns with their existing beliefs. This can further entrench radical ideologies. Social media platforms, through AI-driven content recommendation systems, often create informational silos where users are isolated from opposing viewpoints. This lack of exposure to diverse perspectives can exacerbate extremism, making users more susceptible to radicalization.[10] The confirmation bias reinforced within these echo chambers makes users more confident in the validity of their beliefs, regardless of their factual accuracy. The real-world consequences of these algorithmic decisions can be severe. For example, individuals radicalized on social media have been linked to numerous cases of hate crimes and mass shootings. The algorithms' role in these processes is typically indirect yet potent; by continuously feeding users content that fuels their deepest fears and angers, these systems escalate tensions and can push unstable individuals towards violent action.

Mitigating these issues requires a concerted effort across several fronts. Users must be educated about how algorithms manipulate their content feeds and the potential impacts on their behavior and emotions. Additionally—though unfortunate through the context of government expansion—there might be a need for regulatory measures where governments could step in to regulate the algorithms used by social media companies, ensuring that they promote healthier engagement and prevent the spread of harmful content. Though this has to come heavily with scrutiny, as this could easily tip-toe on the realm of censorship, which has to be avoided at all costs. . . .

Technological solutions could also play a role, with the development of new AI models that prioritize user well-being over simple engagement metrics.[11] Governments could establish guidelines that require social media platforms to make their algorithms more transparent and accountable. One idea might be to reveal parts of the algorithm's code to the public. Additionally, increased public awareness of how these algorithms manipulate emotions and beliefs could spur consumer-driven change.

Ultimately, though, government and the public are powerless, unless we acknowledge that the real change hinges on individual awareness. Without individuals recognizing and knowing how these dynamics affect them personally, government action and public pressure can only go so far. Each person needs to understand that every click, like, and share feeds into and reinforces the algorithms that shape our digital experiences. Engaging with content means you're effectively "voting" for it to be shown more widely, which can perpetuate a cycle of negativity and manipulation.

You, the reader, hold responsibility for your actions and your use of the internet. It's important to be mindful of how you interact with content. By being selective and thoughtful about what you engage with, you can help steer the algorithms toward healthier, more meaningful content, not just for yourself but for others as well. This isn't just about protecting your mental health—it's about safeguarding your overall well-being and, if it resonates with you, your spiritual health too. Every small action counts, and awareness is the first step toward making a meaningful impact.

To combat the rising tide of hate, a multifaceted approach is required. Education is crucial; promoting a comprehensive understanding of history and society can reduce ignorance, a primary feeder of hate. Additionally, fostering economic opportunities for all can help alleviate class resentment. Politically, encouraging bipartisanship and dialogue is essential. Reducing the rhetoric of divisiveness and focusing on common goals can help bridge the vast ideological gaps that have developed. Media reform is also crucial, both in traditional and new media. Promoting responsible journalism and modifying social media algorithms to discourage the spread of hate-filled content are steps in the right direction.

Addressing hate in America involves understanding its root causes and actively working towards a society where differences are respected rather than feared. Tolerance should be practiced from both sides of the aisle, including those who feel they are on the right side of history, or on the right side of the moral spectrum (religious or otherwise). It requires a collective effort across all levels of society—from individual actions to systemic changes—to foster an environment where hate finds no fertile ground to grow.

Reader's Group Discussion Questions

- How does the chapter suggest individual perceptions and personal responsibility contribute to the
  spread or mitigation of hate in society? Discuss
  how personal accountability is portrayed in contrast to the systemic influences mentioned.

- The chapter discusses the impact of social media
  algorithms and mainstream media on amplifying
  divisive content. How do you think these platforms could be redesigned to foster a healthier
  public discourse?

- Economic insecurity and class resentment are
  highlighted as significant contributors to societal
  hate. Discuss the interplay between economic
  conditions and hate. How can society address
  these economic disparities to reduce hate?

- With the example of the 2020 elections and its
  aftermath, the chapter illustrates the depth of political division. What steps could be taken to reduce such polarization? Are there successful examples from history or other countries that could
  guide these efforts?

- The chapter mentions the role of 'Cancel Culture'
  in exacerbating hate. What are the pros and cons
  of Cancel Culture? How does it reflect larger socio-political divisions, and what might be the long-
  term effects on public discourse?

Footnotes:

[1] Müller & Schwarz, 2020. *Journal of the European Economic Association*, Volume 19, Issue 4, August 2021, Pages 2131–2167, https://doi.org/10.1093/jeea/jvaa045

[2] Schneider, Jake, 2022. "We Won't Forget The 'Summer of Love'". https://gop.com/rapid-response/we-wont-forget-the-summer-of-love/

[3] Walker, Jackson. January 8th, 2024. *NBC Montana*. "Biden lauds 2020 BLM riots as 'historic movement for justice' during Monday speech". https://nbc-montana.com/news/nation-world/biden-lauds-2020-blm-riots-as-historic-movement-for-justice-during-monday-speech-mother-emanuel-ame-church-in-charleston-sc-black-lives-matter-george-floyd-summer-of-love-politics-trump-president-white-house-2024-race

[4] Kingson, Jennifer A. (September 16, 2020). "Exclusive: $1 billion-plus riot damage is most expensive in insurance history." Axios. Retrieved October 10, 2020. https://www.axios.com/2020/09/16/riots-cost-property-damage

[5] History.com Editors. May 24th, 2021. *History*. "George Floyd is killed by a police officer, igniting historic protests". https://www.history.com/this-day-in-history/george-floyd-killed-by-police-officer

[6] YouTube User: Associated Press. September 30th, 2020. *YouTube*. "Trump tells Proud Boys: 'Stand back and stand by'". https://www.youtube.com/watch?v=qIHhB1ZMV_o

[7] Ronayne, Kathleen. September 30th, 2020. *AP News*. "Trump to far-right extremists: 'Stand back and stand by'". https://apnews.com/article/election-2020-joe-biden-race-and-ethnicity-donald-trump-chris-wallace-0b32339da25fbc9e8b7c7c7066a1db0f

[8] X User: "@JoeBiden". September 30th, 2020. *X*, formally *Twitter*. https://twitter.com/JoeBiden/status/1311268302950260737?ref_src=twsrc%5Etfw%7Ctwcamp%5Etweetembed%7Ctwterm%5E1311268302950260737%7Ctwgr%5E34a9ed9a0f5beef874fe095e652c2881fe60c07b%7Ctwcon%5Es1_&ref_url=https%3A%2F%2Fadage.com%2Farticle%2Fcampaign-trail%2Fbiden-turns-trumps-proud-boys-debate-moment-campaign-ad%2F2284641

[9] Cochrane, Emily & Broadwater, Luke. February 24th, 2021. *New York Times*. "Capitol Riot Costs Will Exceed $30 Million, Official Tells Congress". https://www.nytimes.com/2021/02/24/us/politics/capitol-riot-damage.html

[10] Bail, C., Argyle, L., Brown, T., Bumpus, J., Chen, H., Hunzaker, M., Lee, J., Mann, M., Merhout, F., & Volfovsky, A. (2018). Exposure to opposing views on social media can increase political polarization. Proceedings of the National Academy of Sciences of the United States of America, 115, 9216 - 9221. https://doi.org/10.1073/pnas.1804840115.

[11] Garland, J., Zahedi, K., Young, J., Hébert-Dufresne, L., & Galesic, M. (2020). Countering hate on social media: Large scale classification of hate and counter speech. ArXiv, abs/2006.01974. https://doi.org/10.18653/v1/2020.alw-1.13.

["nostalgia sickness": the elderly, the younger gener- ation, the good times, the bad times, and why we all cling and yearn for mo- ments we attach to...]

There is a phenomenon that I personally have coined, though it is probably already properly named. "Nostalgia Sickness." It's a feeling that you would know if you felt it. The longing or yearning for a memorable past. "The Golden Era," as you would think in your mind. The era that defined you as a person. Possibly the era of your heyday, when you felt the most complete or the most happy in this world. Everyone, I think, eventually starts to feel it at some point in their life. Some more than others, and some with a higher intensity than others. It's okay to experience nostalgia, and even partake in the market of nostalgia—purchasing items of that time, holding them, cherishing them, and basking in their glory—but what is *not* okay is ruminating about the past so much so that it causes you to lose track of what is happening in The Now, the present moment, modern life. . . .

I think most generations struggle with nostalgia. And the Millennial generation is no stranger to that struggle. For Millennials, nostalgia serves as a means of cultural identity formation. Growing up in an era characterized by rapid technological advancements and socio-cultural shifts, Millennials often find themselves grappling with a sense of disconnection from their roots. Nostalgia, therefore, becomes a way to reconnect with shared cultural touchstones and forge a sense of belonging in an increasingly fragmented world. The prevalence of nostalgia among Millennials also reflects a desire to escape from the complexities and uncertainties of modern life. From economic instability to political upheavals, Millennials have borne witness to a myriad of challenges that have left them yearning for the perceived simplicity of bygone eras—an example being the times before the start of COVID-19. Nostalgia offers a temporary reprieve from the stresses of contemporary existence, allowing individuals to retreat into the comforting embrace of familiar cultural artifacts and memories.

In an age characterized by hyper-connectivity and digital saturation, Millennials often find themselves yearning for authenticity and genuineness. Nostalgia, with its emphasis on the beholder's past, represents a quest for a time when experiences felt more authentic and less curated. Whether it's vinyl records, vintage clothing, or analog photography, Millennials, a whopping 47% of them (while Gen-Z a whopping 50%)[1], are drawn to tangible relics of the past that evoke a sense of nostalgia. And nostalgia authenticity. It particularly hits harder for Millennials, in my opinion, purely because Millennials saw a shift or rise in technological advancement. Moving from the 8-bit video game systems like the DMG-Gameboy from Nintendo to the 64-bit Nintendo 64. The '90s and early 2000s were a huge time for gaming. But not just games, social media as well. Myspace, Friendster, Tumblr, Formspring, Limewire, BearShare, etc. These were all applications on computers that really set a huge mark on the minds of Millennials. It connected best friends in huge ways, making accessibility to features never seen before in our reality. It's easy to create a sense of Nostalgia around a formable and awe-inspiring feeling that no human has ever felt before, especially when a collective generation seemingly felt it in unison.

Motivation for this collective nostalgia varies. The resurgence of nostalgia among Millennials can be attributed to a confluence of socio-cultural, psychological, and technological factors that shape their lived experiences and worldviews. As digital natives who straddle the divide between analog and digital worlds, Millennials navigate a complex landscape characterized by rapid change and constant flux. An article from *Medium* entitled "The Allure of Millennial Nostalgia" gives a perfect reference[2] to the feelings associated with this fleeting and often painful nostalgia that Millennials seem to face:

"The other day, I stumbled upon something in my Instagram Discover feed that stopped me in my tracks. It was an account dedicated entirely to the American Girl Doll catalog from the '90s, which I used to obsess over as a little girl.¶ For me, this discovery was more than just a fleeting moment of online nostalgia; it was a portal to a simpler time in life where my beloved Samantha doll served as a comforting companion through the ups and downs of my childhood—which included the divorce of my parents and an international move to Norway at the age of 12. Sadly, my doll was lost in that move, and I often dream of finding her in a forgotten corner of my parent's attic.¶ As I delved deeper into the account, I couldn't help but feel a rush of memories surging through me. It was like stepping through a time machine, whisking me away to a more innocent world where doll outfits and meticulously crafted furniture sets excited me like nothing else.¶ It took a moment to remember I was in 2023 and now an adult with responsibilities like making sure my taxes are filed on time."

Nostalgia serves as an anchor amidst this uncertainty, offering a sense of continuity and connection to the past. Nostalgia provides psychological comfort and reassurance during times of stress and uncertainty, serving as a coping mechanism for Millennials confronted with the challenges of adulthood. By revisiting cherished memories and cultural artifacts from the past, Millennials derive a sense of security and stability in an otherwise chaotic world. Nostalgia carries cultural significance for Millennials, serving as a bridge between the past and the present, tradition and innovation. By revisiting and reinterpreting elements of the past, Millennials reaffirm their cultural identity and heritage, reclaiming lost narratives and memories that resonate with their lived experiences.

The generation before Millennials, Gen-Xers, have likewise experienced the remnants of a past that is no longer the present case. Between the 1960s and the 1980s, Gen-Xers grew up during a period marked by significant cultural shifts, including the rise of MTV, the emergence of personal computing, and the advent of iconic pop culture phenomena. As a result, they harbor nostalgia for the distinctive cultural artifacts and experiences of their youth, ranging from classic rock music and arcade games to cult TV shows and films. Gen-Xers are often characterized as a generation that rebelled against the norms and conventions of mainstream society, embracing countercultural movements and alternative lifestyles. Their nostalgia is often tinged with a sense of defiance and irony, reflecting their disillusionment with the commercialization of culture and the erosion of authenticity in contemporary society.

Like Millennials, Gen-Xers exhibit a strong affinity for nostalgic media consumption, gravitating towards films, music, and TV shows from their formative years. . . . However, their nostalgia tends to be rooted in the aesthetics and sensibilities of the '70s and '80s, reflecting their unique cultural imprint and generational identity. Despite their smaller cohort size compared to Baby Boomers and Millennials, Gen-Xers have left an indelible mark on popular culture, shaping trends in music, fashion, and entertainment. Their nostalgia reflects a longing for the heyday of alternative rock, grunge fashion, and indie cinema, underscoring their role as cultural influencers and tastemakers.

There is a concept hallmarked with the Trading Card Game (TCG) community. The concept is called "Power Creep." A certain flaw in game balance design, where content released later tends to get more powerful as time goes on. This can be seen in multiplayer games that have regular expansions or balance patches. Power Creep can also refer to the average increase in relative power for all released content in a game.[3] The reason I reference the definition of what a Power Creep is is because we can almost see it in every aspect of our lives. With the advent of digital media and social networking platforms, nostalgia has become more accessible and amplified in contemporary culture. Individuals can easily revisit and share nostalgic content, leading to a broader dissemination and reinforcement of nostalgic sentiments across diverse demographic groups. Brands and marketers have recognized the commercial value of nostalgia and actively leveraged it in advertising, product design, and entertainment. The commodification of nostalgia through retro-themed products, reboots, and remakes contributes to its heightened influence in consumer culture, perpetuating a cycle of nostalgia-driven consumption.

As different generations coexist and interact in an increasingly interconnected global society, nostalgia becomes a shared cultural currency that transcends generational boundaries. Millennials may nostalgically reminisce about '90s pop culture, while Baby Boomers long for the glory days of '60s counterculture, creating a cross-generational dialogue and exchange of nostalgic experiences. In times of social, political, or economic uncertainty, nostalgia offers a comforting refuge and means of escapism for individuals seeking solace in the familiarity of the past. The allure of nostalgia as a form of emotional catharsis contributes to its enduring appeal and potential for intensification over time. While nostalgia itself may not inherently exhibit a linear progression or escalation in *power*, the cultural dynamics surrounding nostalgia can contribute to its amplification and proliferation over time. As society continues to evolve, the role of nostalgia as a cultural force and emotional anchor is likely to remain significant, shaping collective memory and identity in increasingly complex ways.

TCG gaming itself bankrolls on nostalgia, and some would argue it is the defining feature of its allure.[4] It is easy to keep churning out boxes of products every month when you know people in the secondary market are reselling like mad. The biggest sale—and arguably the most famous sale—being a Pokémon card sold to YouTube star Logan Paul for over $5 million.[5] Bankrolling off nostalgia via collectibles, vintage items, and the like, this isn't anything new: It is simple supply and demand. A rare item that is nostalgic and that someone is willing to buy to experience and hold that nostalgia in their hands is big, big money. But it seems that Power Creep in the market is invariably over-saturating the supply. Better cards, cooler designs, and more shiny products. Larger products: bigger, badder, and more rare! It all ties into Power Creep, which at this point appears to be a synonym for progression in all markets, all of life.

The *Los Angeles Times* did an article[6] on the potential investment and value of collectibles that seemed to surge during the pandemic. The Article, titled "Pokémon Cards Are Making Collectors Serious Cash. Some People Are Upset About It," quoted a story from an average Millennial that is very reminiscent of how the pandemic bred a new hunger for nostalgia:

> Anthony Jimenez hadn't thought much about his Pokémon cards since middle school, when girls suddenly seemed more interesting.¶ But with time on his hands during the pandemic, Jimenez dug out his old collection and found that the cards were in pristine condition, a fact that would change his life and financial outlook.¶ "When I found my old Pokémon cards, it was like, 'Oh my God, these are skyrocketing in value. I should try to sell some of them,'" Jimenez said. "So we decided, just for fun, to try this out because L.A. was shut down, and we literally had nothing to do."

COVID-19, the year of 2020, kept the entire nation indoors for a prolonged period. It left individuals who would otherwise be working, going to bars or events, or spending time with friends and family, to explore their attics and old documents that they have been putting off for ages. During the pandemic, Depression and Anxiety increased by 25%, according to the World Health Organization (WHO).[7] This begs the question if there is a correlation with socially withdrawing from the world and whether it has an effect on the human mind. It could, quite possibly, encourage you to free up time and ruminate on things from your past. Old video games, collectibles, Pokemon cards, and the like . . . And maybe it could even spark so-called "Nostalgia Sickness." When the world crumbled like it did in 2020, it can make you long for a forgotten past that you didn't know was so gravy and so enjoyable. This concept came full force towards everyone during the pandemic, not just Gen-Zers and Millennials.

Missing our formidable years and longing for them to come back isn't healthy in the least. But do you blame someone for feeling that way? When you have a generation who is less financially stable than their own parents at their age, a generation whose only real source of dating and companionship seems to stem from online dating hook-up culture, college hook-up culture, and Instagram feeds flooded with OnlyFans models, it shapes the generation for failure. The prospect of owning a home—or owning anything of value for that matter—is seemingly long gone . . . or the looming possibility that you will work for the remainder of your life doing menial and purpose-less tasks for corporations that just see you as a number in their HR department. These are concepts that will break down the spirit of any individual. Hopelessness can happen to anyone, but it surely can happen when your honest reality showcases zero light at the end of the tunnel. When it's possible to look back at said tunnel for tiny snippets of light, it makes nostalgia and such ideas easy to partake in and long for.

While it seems relatively uncouth in this format/medium to disclose my personal tastes—and my struggles with my own moments of nostalgia—I would like to share with you a favorite song of mine that always takes me back. A song that makes me nostalgic for the days of skateboarding in Middle School, riding around and being a hoodlum on the streets of West Palm Beach, Florida. Early-2000s. A time of freedom for me. Hearing this song by Modest Mouse, "The Ocean Breathes Salty," originally released August 23rd, 2004, as their second single from their fourth studio album, gives me great pleasure hearing it on my days driving home from work. Give it a listen:

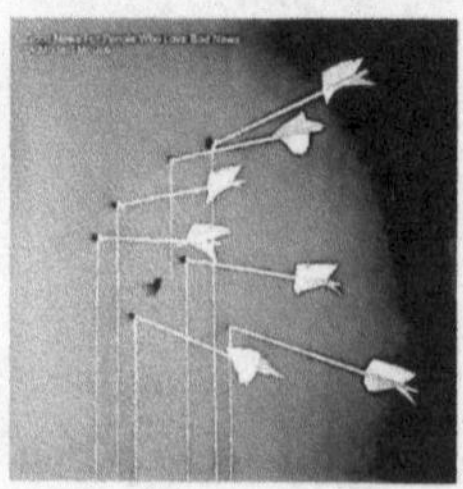

Artist: **Modest Mouse**
Song: **"Ocean Breathes Salty"**
Album: <u>**Good**</u> <u>**News**</u> <u>**for**</u> <u>**People**</u> <u>**Who**</u> <u>**Love**</u> <u>**Bad**</u> <u>**News**</u>
Label: **Epic Records**
Release date: **April 6th, 2004**

Reader's Group Discussion Questions

- Have you experienced nostalgia sickness? How does this concept resonate with your personal experiences of longing for the past?

- How do you see nostalgia affecting different generations differently, especially considering technological and cultural shifts?

- In what ways has nostalgia shaped your cultural identity or that of your peers? Can you identify specific cultural artifacts or moments that trigger these feelings?

- Can nostalgia be considered purely beneficial, or does it have potential negative effects on our ability to live in the present?

- How has the internet and social media influenced the spread and intensity of nostalgic feelings among different age groups?

- Discuss the phenomenon of collectibles and nostalgia-driven consumption. How do you view the market dynamics that capitalize on nostalgic sentiments?

- What are some ways we can honor our past and the nostalgia we feel without letting it hinder our present and future experiences?

Footnotes:

[1] Harlow, Stephanie. March 2nd, 2023. *GWI.* "How are Gen Z and millennials driving nostalgia?". https://blog.gwi.com/trends/nostalgia-trend/

[2] L.O., Kelsey. September 28th, 2023. *Medium.* "The Allure of Millennial Nostalgia". https://kelseylo.medium.com/the-allure-of-millennial-nostalgia-5c8d169c60f3

[3] Username: "Spudthespud". May 30th, 2018. *Urban Dictionary.* "Power Creep" Definition. https://www.urbandictionary.com/define.php?term=Power%20Creep

[4] Fairbrother, Logan. September 22nd, 2023. *Hypebeast.* "From Concept to Card: The Magic Behind 'Pokémon TCG'". https://hypebeast.com/2023/9/pokemon-tcg-151-barry-sams-interview

[5] Teije, Iris Ten. May 17th, 2022. *Forbes.* "How Investors Are Turning Nostalgia Into Profits". https://www.forbes.com/sites/forbesfinancecouncil/2022/05/17/how-investors-are-turning-nostalgia-into-profits/?sh=46c0071f756d

[6] White, Ronald D., Staff Writer. August 23rd., 2021. *LA Times.* "Pokémon cards are making collectors serious cash. Some people are upset about it". https://www.latimes.com/business/story/2021-08-23/covid-era-pokemon-collectibles-demand-surge-causes-problems

[7] Unknown Author. March 2nd, 2022. *World Health Organization.* "COVID-19 pandemic triggers 25% increase in prevalence of anxiety and depression worldwide". https://www.who.int/news/item/02-03-2022-covid-19-pandemic-triggers-25-increase-in-prevalence-of-anxiety-and-depression-worldwide

["gen-z & beyond…": what we can foresee in the future if we remain on our present trajectory—and "can it be fixed?"]

Gen-Z is slowly but surely taking over the conversation as it pertains to the next prominent youthful generation—as expected, due to them being next in line after Millennials. They have a role in taking the baton in both the workforce and in the country's cultural conversation. This, fortunately, is normal in regard to societal evolution. It's the next step in the aging process. Ask yourself this question: *Can I trust Gen-Z, the next generation after Millennials, to handle the future workforce, responsibilities, and progress in our culture?* Can we guess they will cope and progress the world for the better? If the answer is no, you have to have a strong solution to fix that.

Unfortunately, if it was easy to fix, though, it would have already been implemented. With the way technology and culture is evolving, so too is our ignorance of a possible solution. Concepts like mass communication through social media are wholeheartedly new to the human psyche—and with that power comes unforeseen consequences.

Could it be that this reluctance is an indication of growing pains for an ever-changing future? Time will tell. Maybe—just maybe—they will take the baton swimmingly and further push the progress of our future. But not to be grim or pessimistic, with the rapid change Millennials have shown in regards to a generational evolution, it is extremely hard to tell what is in store for the future.

Fortunately (or unfortunately), as politics and government policy move forward, so too are the inevitable rewards or repercussions that save face—often in the same way repeated policies were tried in the past. To learn from history is to learn with present wisdom. Sometimes we are doomed to repeat the same mistakes because new generations forget (and/or have no knowledge of) why the mistakes happened in the first place, and why exactly they are even labeled *mistakes* to begin with. It takes repeating history to learn from history—a necessary refresher, if you will.

I like to think back to the early 1900s, all the way up to the 1950s: We experienced World War I (1914-1918), known as the Great War, involving the world's great powers and was one of the deadliest conflicts in history. Then the Spanish Flu Pandemic (1918-1919), where, following World War I, this pandemic resulted in the deaths of millions of people worldwide. Undoubtedly one of the deadliest pandemics in human history (resulted in an estimated 50 million deaths worldwide, with some estimates going as high as 100 million, while COVID-19 resulted in 6 million deaths worldwide). The Great Depression (1929-1939), a severe worldwide economic disaster that took a heavy toll and devastated the lives of our American society. It was the longest, deepest, and most widespread depression of the 20th century. Then World War II and the Holocaust (1939-1945), where we saw the horrific effects that fascism and ethnic cleansing had on the world. It was the deadliest conflict in human history. The Start of the Cold War (1947-1991), the Atomic bombing of Hiroshima and Nagasaki (1945), and the list goes on and on. . . . These histories are things we have to (and should) always remember and learn from.

As Americans (and as humans), we are damned resilient, as history has both proved and shown. The true weakness that we as a society are experiencing is both our curse and our blessing: Technology. Our lives are much easier to navigate, but also the competition, greed, and overall fast pace living is moving us in a rapid direction towards a whirlwind of chaos—though this is only my personal opinion. With the change we see unfolding, where technology redefines our every step and history's lessons loom large, the question of Gen-Z's capacity to navigate the future becomes not just a matter of trust, but of collective effort. It is easy to fall into the trap of skepticism, to doubt the capabilities of the next generation based on the tumultuous path we've all tread. Yet, it is crucial to remember that each generation is shaped not only by the challenges it faces but by the legacy it inherits.

Gen-Z stands at the threshold of a future that is both daunting and ripe with potential. Armed with the lessons of the past and the tools of the modern age, they possess an unprecedented opportunity to steer our society toward a more enlightened course. The rapid pace of technological advancement and the mistakes of generations past offer both a cautionary tale and a blueprint for innovation. It is through acknowledging our historical missteps and leveraging our technological prowess for the greater good that progress is forged. The resilience of the human spirit, as evidenced by our journey through the harrows of the 20th century, underscores our capacity to overcome adversity. Gen-Z, like the generations before it, is imbued with this indomitable spirit. Their journey is buoyed by a wealth of knowledge and connectivity that previous generations could scarcely imagine. This digital native generation is poised to harness the power of technology not as a harbinger of chaos but as a tool for unity, understanding, and global betterment. This is everything we can hope for—and it will happen.

The responsibility then falls not solely on Gen-Z but on all of us, to guide, support, and collaborate with the next generation. It is through fostering a culture of mentorship, encouraging critical thinking, and promoting empathy that we can truly unlock the potential of the future. The challenges we face as a society—environmental crisis, inequalities, looming inflation, the economy, poor educational systems, crumbling infrastructure, huge division on Capital Hill, and the ethical dilemmas posed by technological advancement—demand a collective response. Gen-Z, with their fresh perspectives and inherent connectivity, are well-equipped to lead this charge, but their success is contingent upon the wisdom and experience of those who came before. . . .

As we stand on the precipice of the future, let us choose to view the uncertainty not with fear but with optimism. The trials and triumphs of the past century have demonstrated our capacity to confront the unthinkable and emerge stronger. With Gen-Z at the helm, supported by the collective wisdom of millennia, the future holds the promise of innovation, unity, and progress. It is a future that can be shaped for the better, should we choose to face it not as disparate generations but as a unified society, eager to learn from our past and forge a path of enlightened progress. . . . Though it should be point-blank said that in the end, the legacy of Gen-Z will be determined not by their ability to avoid the mistakes of the past but by their willingness to engage with them—to learn, adapt, and envision a future that reflects the best of human potential.

None of us are perfect. No generation will ever claim that. But as Gen-Zers take the supposed baton of our country's future, let us offer them not skepticism but support, not doubt but hope, and not isolation but the wisdom of collective experience. Together, we can move towards a future where technology and humanity converge in harmony, where the lessons of the past illuminate the path forward, and where the next generation is empowered to lead with resilience, empathy, and innovation. Together, across generations, we stand at the dawn of a new era, poised to paint a future where every voice is heard, every dream valued, and every challenge met with unwavering courage and collaboration. God bless the world. God bless the United States of America.

Reader's Group Discussion Questions

- Considering the transition from Millennials to Gen-Z, how do you perceive the readiness of Gen-Z to address and navigate the complex challenges outlined in the chapter?

- The chapter presents technology as both society's greatest asset and its potential downfall. Reflect on this dual-edged nature of technological advancement. How can society leverage technology for positive change while mitigating its risks?

- The chapter draws parallels between the past century's tumultuous events and today's challenges. What lessons from the historical events mentioned do you think are most pertinent for Gen-Z?

- The author emphasizes a unified approach to shaping the future, suggesting that responsibility lies with all generations. In what ways can different generations contribute to a more promising future, and how can these contributions be harmonized?

- The conclusion of the chapter calls for offering Gen-Z support, hope, and collective wisdom. Discuss the impact of optimism and support on societal progress. How can individuals and communities provide meaningful support to the next generation in practical terms?

Recommended Reading

- "Can't Even: How Millennials Became the Burnout Generation" by Anne Helen Petersen

- "Broke Millennial: Stop Scraping By and Get Your Financial Life Together" by Erin Lowry

- "Americanah" by Chimamanda Ngozi Adichie

- "The Subtle Art of Not Giving a F*ck: A Counterintuitive Approach to Living a Good Life" by Mark Manson

- "Your Brain on Porn: Internet Pornography and the Emerging Science of Addiction" by Gary Wilson

- "Atlas Shrugged" by Ayn Rand

- "The Art of Fielding" by Chad Harbach

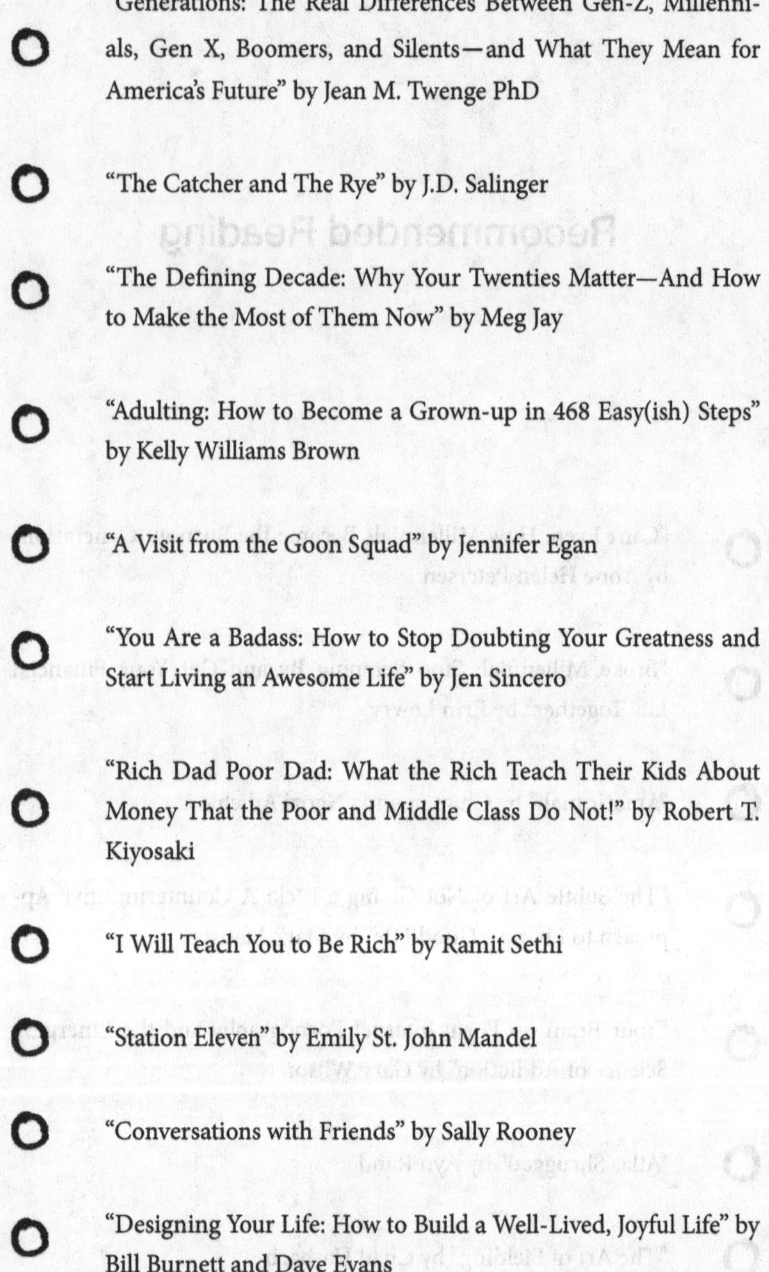

"Generations: The Real Differences Between Gen-Z, Millennials, Gen X, Boomers, and Silents—and What They Mean for America's Future" by Jean M. Twenge PhD

"The Catcher and The Rye" by J.D. Salinger

"The Defining Decade: Why Your Twenties Matter—And How to Make the Most of Them Now" by Meg Jay

"Adulting: How to Become a Grown-up in 468 Easy(ish) Steps" by Kelly Williams Brown

"A Visit from the Goon Squad" by Jennifer Egan

"You Are a Badass: How to Stop Doubting Your Greatness and Start Living an Awesome Life" by Jen Sincero

"Rich Dad Poor Dad: What the Rich Teach Their Kids About Money That the Poor and Middle Class Do Not!" by Robert T. Kiyosaki

"I Will Teach You to Be Rich" by Ramit Sethi

"Station Eleven" by Emily St. John Mandel

"Conversations with Friends" by Sally Rooney

"Designing Your Life: How to Build a Well-Lived, Joyful Life" by Bill Burnett and Dave Evans

O "Man's Search for Meaning" by Viktor E. Frankl

O "Big Magic: Creative Living Beyond Fear" by Elizabeth Gilbert

O "The Marriage Plot" by Jeffrey Eugenides

O "The Life-Changing Magic of Tidying Up: The Japanese Art of Decluttering and Organizing" by Marie Kondo

O "The Circle" by Dave Eggers

O "How Not to Die: Discover the Foods Scientifically Proven to Prevent and Reverse Disease" by Michael Greger

O "Atomic Habits: An Easy & Proven Way to Build Good Habits & Break Bad Ones" by James Clear

O "Normal People" by Sally Rooney

O "Society Of The Spectacle" by Guy Debord

AUTHOR CONTACT INFORMATION

Instagram —————— **@kevinklix**
X, formally *Twitter* —— **@kevinklix**
E-mail — **kevinklix@yahoo.com**
TikTok ———————— **@klitztopher**

PHOTO BY CASEY MILNER-KNOTTS

About the Author:

Kevin Klix lives and works in West Palm Beach, Florida with his girlfriend, Casey. He has written six novels, two self-helps, two non-fiction, and one collection of poetry. He enjoys writing on his typewriter, where he makes frequent poetry posts on his Instagram (@kevinklix). He does ink drawings, digital/film photography, and he plays Blues on his electric guitar when he has free time.

Read on for an excerpt from

Beautiful Nihilism

An Unconventional Conservative's Collection of Essays

Available wherever books are sold

The Paradox Called Living

I wasn't lonely. I experienced no self-pity. I was just caught up in a life in which I could find no meaning.

— CHARLES BUKOWSKI

If I told you that I know the true answer to the beginning of life, would you allow me to spew that piece of information to you? Would you not want to know? or would you say my claim is nonsense and can never, ever truly be possible? You would most-likely be both right and wrong — but I frankly don't blame you in all three instances.

You may say to yourself, "How arrogant of this essayist to suggest that he knows such a completely outlandish answer! How pretentious!" And hey, I don't particularly blame you, but it's actually quite simpler than that. Here, let me explain: We have this existing concept called *nominal world*. It's the idea of an external universe or existence without life, the outside life from any mind; henceforth, inanimate objects, planets, star-dust, dark matter, all crazy, out-there concepts balled up into one that you have heard a million, zillion times before in the scientific community. That, my friends, cannot be answered on how that started because that is not considered *Life*. What is life then? Let's define it.

Life, to me, is a generation of bio-organisms that function on a path of both survival and making copies of itself. That is their only purpose, and that, my friends, is what every single living creature you have ever come across's goal is in life: your mother, father, your dog, your boss, your long-lost uncle Jeffrey, plants, whoever it is or whatever it is has that one very simple goal. Though it is a superficial goal that nobody in their right mind would directly identify with, it is the ultimate reason for most motives in life; that, along with making the entire process as easy and as comfortable as possible. But living and consciousness are not one in the same, and here's why.

Think of your body as *nominal world* and your consciousness being the life created from it. There is Nominal World, then Life, then Consciousness. Through consciousness something else breeds besides simply survival and procreation: *Purpose*. Purpose is the tool used to mask the ultimate life goal of survival and procreation. Things such as morals, policies, laws, good and evil, right and wrong, et cetera, are all tied into purpose to create the illusion of the ultimate goal of all life-forms.

In a space devoid of life it is mostly stardust, dark matter, and basically "nothingness." But how, you might say, can something such as stardust or dark matter or anything material for that matter not be considered *something*. The reason being is it takes consciousness to even make it exist. To see it is to create it. In a world such as this, it is extremely easy for life to be created, with of course the right conditions such as a sizable star with a not-so-sizable planet to have things such as vitality, water, temperature, atmosphere . . . so on and so forth.

In this sense, the very concept of nothingness is simply changed to the idea of a life without consciousness. Without consciousness, that is nothingness. And that is what my answer is on the start of life. . . . Case closed? Hardly. Most who read or hear this type of answer will ask: *But what started space, the universe, the stardust, everything "non-living"?* That's when the question gets interesting because you are not asking how life got started but how the start of a start can possibly occur.

A paradox! It is the ultimate question of debate that has stumped humanity since the beginning of Life itself. It is the reason we have thousands of religions and theories and deities. Some would argue it's the reason to even live in the first place to find out the ultimate answer to that question. Regardless of why, inside the conscious mind of a living being, more specifically a *homo sapien* being, is the deepest yearning in gaining a *fully-grasped objective reality*, material or non-material.

Will we ever obtain the answer to that ultimate life question? Sadly, I would have to say no. It's not in the cards for us because, as of right now, in this part of our evolutionary stage we each have a limited mind with limited senses. Even our eyes can only see a small fraction of wavelengths. Our ears are not nearly as good as dogs, for example. Our taste is muted compared to dogs too. Not to say dogs, or any animal for that matter, are "superior"; it's to say that we have a long way to go before ever having the tools to accurately be able to answer a colossal kind of question: the ultimate last question that defines everything.

Scientists often look at the idea of consciousness. What is it? What's *unconsciousness?* The only way to even know somewhat closely to what unconsciousness is — without of course going against everything nature tells us and is quite frankly the exact opposite of life itself — is to close your eyes and imagine you not being here, you not even knowing of being or your ego. You before you were born, that kind of nothingness. People cannot stand the idea of being dead or simply just not being alive anymore. Forget death, let's just talk about not being alive first. Before birth, we never had consciousness; we weren't floating around asking ourselves when we will be eventually conscious and when we will go to this place called Planet Earth. It wasn't there. It didn't exist. Consciousness is everything to the ego and to the Self.

Death is simply the *loss of consciousness.* People ask what happens when you die, and scientist seem to gravitate towards what will happen to their remains, that if and when they die, flora and fauna will rise once again and consume them for the next life to blossom. The cycle of life, in other words. . . . But when we think or ask what happens *at* death, we are asking what is happening to the individual consciousness upon death and what happens to *them* in that process. I understand that utter chaos and conundrum the idea of death is — I, too, as a fellow human being alongside you, am scared beyond reason of death and what it will be — but there are many things that can happen that simply will rid yourself of discomfort. Right now, the thought of death produces fear and discomfort. If consciousness were to cease, there is zero comfort or discomfort. It's muted. The "energy" is ceased. Other animals have been influenced by you. Even crossing the street and someone seeing you on the side of the road influences a person. They will think, "I have to yield to my fellow man if I want him to live! I do not want him to die because I know that if I were in *his* position — which I know can very well happen to me — I, too, would want him to do the same and yield to me!" Obviously, the thought is not in that literal process, but it is the ultimate sub-conscious behavior. It shows compassion, integrity, and growth in another person's mind, simply by you just existing. The face — or to see another face — is something we take for granted: It is a *need*. Anyone isolated and sensory-deprived will tell you that.

We are living inside of this beautiful, ugly, baffling reality, where nothing is certain and only a small fraction of things can be fully answered with complete objective truth. All things point to a world of paradoxes. Any and all debates have them; one cannot be fully absolute, including me, as I often stumble into absolutism simply by being a living human-being. So I ask again: *What if I told you the true answer to the beginning of life?* The truly objective answer is: "I don't know." There is no point to bring meaning into it. You have to let that go and just live it as best you can.

Chapter 1 — Group or individual topic questions:

✓ Knowing that you are a mortal being, what would you do if you could know everything in the world as if you had been alive since the beginning of time?

✓ Do you fear the idea of immortality more than you fear the idea of death?

✓ If you knew definitive proof of life after death, and it was an absolute utopia, would you be anxious to want to die?

✓ Can utopias sustain themselves when free individuals are present?

✓ If a robot were crossing the street, one without consciousness of you, would you yield to it the same way you would yield to a human-being?

✓ Can you imagine what "nothingness" would be like without picturing the absolute of it? By this I mean can multiple factors come into play?

✓ Do you think that spirits exist inside the human body, despite what scientist believe?

✓ What would space be without a life-form to consciously observe it? Objects floating around in an abyss? What could get done? Would "getting done" even matter?

✓ In a world devoid of life, does meaning exist? Can inanimate objects have meaning? Or better yet, can unconscious, lifeless objects have meaning?

✓ If life is actually meaningless, how does that make you feel? Sad? Angry? Depressed beyond all reason? Does it strip you of any hopes, dreams, or motivation? Would it make you think to succumb to "meaningless," "hedonistic" pleasures (drugs, sex, crime, eating, sloth, et cetera)?

CHAPTER TWO

Religious Nihilism

*If we believe in nothing, if nothing has any meaning and if we
can affirm no values whatsoever, then everything is possible and
nothing has any importance.*

— ALBERT CAMUS

Nihilism is generally seen in a dark light, but I feel, as an advocate of Nihilism's principals, I should bring to the forefront some information that may so-called "un-stigmatize" the philosophy, just a tad. Firstly, when viewing life as meaningless, it is common in human condition to also feel as though that *they* are meaningless, that the *individual* is pushed entirely inward and a sudden, oddly ominous feeling of dread and/or anxiety overwhelms the individual, sometimes together simultaneously.

With this initial response to life's perceived appearance of "meaninglessness" — as Albert Camus would call "the Absurd" — it is understandable for anyone, especially people external to the individual feeling these symptoms, to write it off as something that they would want to avoid at all costs whenever possible — and ultimately to not think about.

I'm not going to say that anyone who feels this way towards the philosophy is right or wrong, because just me even advocating absolute feeling as "good" or "bad" discredits me as a nihilist; but what I *am* saying is that as a collective society any feeling of dread, anxiety, unhappiness, or anything else perceived as "negative" is always going to be perceived as "bad," because the very essence of a meaning is having "hopes & dreams," goals & desires, and any negative feelings are simply the body's natural response to it perceiving itself *not being on the right track* to whatever perceived meaning (or, i.e., "hopes, dreams, goals, and desires") it has.

If you watch a debate between a Republican and a Democrat, the majority of people feel that their policies are under the guise of helping society for the greater good . . . But are they really? Sure, they both believe in the core of their hearts that they are helping others, but the debate is empty most of the time. Any controversial subject is only subjectively controversial because either the problem is seen as morally wrong (typically Conservatives feeling that way), or it's a matter of rights (typically Liberals . . .) in both instances, the same result occurs: the issue discussed is an issue that cannot be solved easily and effortlessly on a majority agreement basis (bipartisan). Lots of people add to the pot and place in their two cents.

What I find is that you can have the most interesting debate when you merge together two logics that contradict each other. For example, abortion. To conservatives: if you are pro-life, and a pregnant immigrant comes into the United States of America illegally and their baby grants them government assistance, is that going to conflict your pro-life views (assuming you have a democratic president who controls the assistance budget)? That's when you have an interesting debate. Or how about Liberals: if you are pro-choice — even pro-choice all the way up to the end of the 9-months — knowing that notoriously women that have abortions, especially Dilation & Extraction (D&E) abortions at the first or second trimester of the pregnancy, is it going to end up giving them overall feelings of sadness (possibly guilt too) and end up begging the question if that is "liberating" for women to have abortions that late? or if it actually defeats them?

Often in a debate they, Conservatives and Liberals, give cherry-picked examples of instances that back their views, and when you give examples or alternative possibilities, they will often laugh and say, "That'll never happen." Well, my friends, being as the USofA has hundreds of millions of people, literally anything has a possibility of happening, and when you implement so-called "controversial" policies for the betterment of society, you also have to look at the possibility of any errors in your decision-making. You see, my philosophy is that all of it is ultimately meaningless (though the pursuit isn't), because no matter what you do you cannot stop anyone from doing anything — we know this because we have more criminals in the United States than any other country (but we also have a lot more population than most . . . but I digress).

Taking into account the meaninglessness of it all, and the ultimate object of people debating and fighting and ultimately not solving anything, I have come to the conclusion that it is never a "good" thing, in my personal opinion, to be full-blown right-wing or full-blown left-wing — you must find a middle ground, whenever possible. You see, to me, politics will always have flaws and errors in any policy, regardless of what it is. The ultimate object is making a policy that minimizes the most errors while still being morally "right," logical to true, objective stats, and caters to the majority masses both on the right and left together. In the question of abortion, for example, my views are somewhat pro-choice and somewhat pro-life, but for many different reasons than most.

Firstly, my belief is that abortion should only be reserved for the first trimester. The reason I say this is because, though I am somewhat pro-choice, I am not an advocated or supporter of D&E abortions. The reason is because often D&E abortions only are necessary when the baby is too big or too far in development, which means oftentimes it has a heartbeat, fingers, toes, a brain, nerves, feelings, and an overall "shape" of a possible living, "breathing" human-being. The concept of D&E is pretty much throwing everything (all concepts of morality) out the window, appeasing just the customer (i.e., the [usually left-leaning] mother), not caring about the thing inside her's life at all, and just forcing that baby to die in the most gruesome way possible: by ripping and yanking them out of its mother, piece by piece.

Though we cannot verify the actual consciousness of the baby in that moment because the baby cannot communicate its own consciousness *to* us, we can only go by imagination of such consciousness by placing ourselves in the baby's shoes, which is not necessarily good or bad, it's just a natural reaction when viewing the essence of this issue. I succumb to this action despite knowing consciously that I do not know for sure the true, objective consciousness of the baby (considering that we know that a majority of people do not remember anything as a tiny infant . . . but I digress). The point is is that when we are ripping apart the baby, and the doctors have the baby's body in front of them, and they are required to piece them back together on a table in front of them to verify that they did, in fact, get all of the baby out of the mother, I find this to fit the same visual not as *medical* but as *murder;* thusly, D&E, to me, unless the baby is going to cause harm to the mother or her life, should be condemned, even by pro-choicers.

So, first-trimester-only abortions. There are some that fall under D&E in this stage of the pregnancy (typically towards the end of the trimester), obviously since every baby has different growth rates, but this is less common, and therefore, though I'm against D&E, I have to look past that minority for the majority's favor. Most first-term pregnancies use a method called Aspiration (suction), Dilation & Curettage (D&C). Though I am a man writing this and that inevitably will grant me backlash, I feel that if the baby is able to fit in a suction tube and is able to be aborted not piece by piece but by flushing or sucking the baby out of the mother like blowing your nose or the common cold, it is likely that that baby not only doesn't appear to take the look of a baby but probably isn't even aware of itself or its existence. This method is later in the first trimester. The earlier, the better . . . and by "better," I mean less "gruesome." The early method (typically under 10 weeks of the pregnancy) is the mother taking two types of pills, Mifepristone and Misoprostol.

Mifepristone blocks the hormone called progesterone,

which brings stabilization of the lining in the mother's uterus. When this is blocked, the baby cannot flourish and then ceases to function. With the dead baby inside, the mother then takes Misoprostol orally or vaginally, which causes the mother to have heavy bleeding contractions that flush the dead baby out of the mother's body. She's in pain, at home, usually, on the toilet when the baby is flushed out, blood coming out of her. At 9 weeks, the baby is an inch long, which is pretty much the size of your thumb — hardly what I would consider to be a resemblance of an actual human. The mother can see this abortion — even hold it — and do whatever she feels fit to do with the dead, genderless organism. (Burial or funeral (if they want to), flushing down the toilet, bring to doctor, et cetera.) In this way, I do not know why I have this feeling in my brain, but I don't view this as actual murder because it's operated and handled more as a medical condition than as an actual pregnancy or dismantlement of a baby (as hypocritical as I sound right now).

In this sense, there would be appeasement of most on the Right and Left. Obviously both can disagree with my views, and that's fine, but in this sense, they both ultimately win whilst still somehow remaining moral if you define an inch, genderless dead life-form to be "human." In this sense, I feel that if someone is having sex, especially unprotected sex, they always are running a risk of ending up being a mother or father and should both make efforts to stay on top of that first-trimester threshold. Things like pregnancy tests, morning-after pills, using and checking condoms (if damaged), making sure to keep track of menstrual cycles, et cetera. In this sense, it makes sexually active people more cautious, which is always a good thing in hindsight.

What about rape? Even then, threshold, legal action, et cetera. Who pays for it? In instances of rape or the mother being medically necessary to have an abortion to save her life, insurance should cover that, or a fund specific to this happening, and then legally being able as the state or insurance company to go after payment (in the instance of rape and the criminal being caught), but never from the mother (besides insurance premiums and deductibles, et cetera). But, if out of choice because of whatever her reason is, out of pocket for the mother and/or the father. The reason being is to make it that much more important for both the mother and father (if not a criminal towards her) to take caution.

But why am I explaining this to tell you about Nihilism and its "morality"? I mean, maybe I'm wrong and don't know every instance of anything to do with abortion and I'm just talking outside of my hoo-ha. . . . But it does beg the question that each and every opinion or view on any subject or debate is ultimately meaningless because no matter what you think, the individuals involved in the actual situation of the debate are going to do whatever they have to do to make sure they appease what their desire is in the matter, legal or illegal. Ultimately, considering morality can only be controlled from you and your own personal life and not other's lives, it is meaningless to debate, because there is no answer when you have paradoxes to the debate; henceforth, "controversial." Always advocate your opinion, though, because progress is always "good" in the sense of two things: survival and procreation, the ultimates of life's goals.

Progress? But doesn't the very idea of pursuing the idea of "progress" mean that life has meaning? This is the big question that defines Nihilism. The answer: *No.* The reason why: because since there is an endless amount of ideologies, and since there is an endless amount of life multiplying and having its own specific goals, intentions, morality, deterministic paths, and not a single spread of actual absolutist objectivity, there is never going to be meaning in the nominal world outside of life: an aimless, inanimate existence can never have consciousness, and to prove that consciousness exists simply by having "conscious" beings say it is because they "feel" it is is never going to be enough to the *unconscious* universe, whatever it is. The universe is aimless and has no goals or desires. It has no right or wrong in it. If a meteor just so happens to hit something and it perpetuates life or destroys life, stepping back you have to realize that that object had nothing of conscious power. And nothing implies no meaning.

This being said, meaning comes, and is only reserved for, so-called "conscious" life-forms, a huge paradox. Knowing the very existence of a paradox should not produce feelings of dread but, instead, feelings of freedom to be a conscious object, a deterministic object that runs into choices or instances that lead it to future choices, and past choices influencing those future choices forever. After all, it has been proven that we already know our choices before we are consciously aware of them . . . so, in that sense, ask yourself this question: *How different am I from the rock that hits something and perpetuates life or destroys it?* Hardly any difference, if you ask me. Let your life flow. Live it fully and don't let negatives overtake you, because it does not progress your existence. But know it's meaningless and know how great it is precisely *because* it's meaningless.

✓   Does the idea of meaninglessness scare you? If it does, why? If it doesn't, why not?

✓   Would meaninglessness change your life or overall quality of life?

✓   If you knew that there was (or wasn't) a higher power, what would be the first thing you would do?

✓   Does "meaning" motivate you?

✓   If you couldn't die, would you still be motivated to do the things you do now? Would you have a sense of urgency?

✓   In a life without consciousness — i.e., the life of a vegetable — would it be possible to have meaning despite being unconscious? Yes or no, why do you think that is so?

✓   If you could describe who you are without saying job title, race, gender, religious views, or the stripping away of any social structure, could you still answer that question effectively?

✓ What is the difference in meaning between animate and inanimate existences?

✓ In your words, what would you consider to be "conscious"?

✓ If something is unconscious, does it have rights? And by that I mean besides the something sharing your same species — inanimate, animate, rocks, stardust, frogs, dogs, humans, anything.

✓ What defines rights and meaning? Is the only authority a higher power to decide such a thing and define its value?

✓ What is your personal meaning in life? (*This you can ponder for a while. No rush.*)

Read on for an excerpt from

Skateboy *A Novel*

Available wherever books are sold

mid-2001

A child's toy consumed my life.

It started the day a friend of mine, Cody, told me that YMCA's ramps were big. He dragged me along on his little "find-out" mission when I was, at the time, nine years old, going to Palm Springs Elementary School. It was there that I met my said friend, Cody. It was Cody's birthday. He was turning ten years old. Cody was into skateboarding, just a little. He dabbled but wasn't very good. He wanted to celebrate his birthday, just him and I, at the skatepark. So I guess that was the thing to do.

The day was very sunny, I remember. It was like the Florida sun was shining down pure rays of positivity—or a stifling, overabundance of heat if you look at it pessimistically. I remember there was a kid there; he had to've been only about four-five. I wasn't much taller, but still, Cody was five-foot and I was hella shorter than he was. The shortness of the kid, well, it had an edge. He had style, like he owned the place, and that I could respect in a kid, even at the time.

At first he was riding down those ramps like a damn monkey. Ooo-Oo-*eEee-AH!* That sort of monkey. He wore this crazy black & white striped shirt and some Walmart shorts. I was sitting on a bench under a pavilion with Cody, my mother on the phone off somewhere in the background.

"Cody," I said. "That kid!"

"Yeah, I see him. Wanna move up closer?"

"Heck yes!" And I did. Cody followed.

I had my face up to the chain-link face, my fingers curling around the wire.

"Dude! That *kid* . . . Holy *crap!*" My eyes were huge, looking back and forth while this kid was just charging at the ramps.

Then, get this: the kid went up this kicker—which, if you are not a skateboarder, is an incline or decline you go up or down—launched in the air (the board staying under him), and landed on top of a four-foot tall railing just ahead of the kicker, glided along it, then finally dropped off and landed down on the cement. Perfectly.

It was love at first sight.

I whirled around and yelled at my mother.

"Mom! I want to be a skateboarder!"

Lo and behold, I became one.

Cody and I lost touch. What a pity.

●　　●　　●

Next day I went through every nook and cranny of my closet. "No, not here," I was saying to myself. "Nope. Not there, either." And then I found it. "YES!" I found a Walmart board, bought five years prior when I was probably four years of age. It had cobwebs on it. The wheels didn't move much. They were plastic, not polyurethane.

So I went outside the front of my house (which was a trailer home, yeah—but pretty nice actually) and set the board down on the asphalt. Scary. I didn't really have many friends, much luck with being cool, or much confidence in sports because I was so damn short. So standing on this piece of wood with a turning mechanism and four wheels . . .

Well, it was scary, I'll tell you that much.

My mother came outside to tan, but to also look after her little geeky boy about to go stepping onto a little, geeky, Walmart board, "the most dangerous of dangers," she said.

I fell immediately when I stood on top of it. I put one foot on, then the other. WHOOPS! It slid right from under me.

"MY BABY!" my mother yelled. "OH, *NO!* MY BABY!"

She started running toward the street. Then she picked me up by one arm from the ground.

"Are you okay, honey? I saw that fall!" She didn't think I was brave enough to be able to do a sport.

I just smiled. "That was awesome," I said.

Then, a second try: I set the board back down on the cement, took a deep breath, and stood on top of the board.

That second time I didn't fall.

• • •

My mother brought me lessons at the YMCA. She wanted me to be taught "professionally," which I now know is not *really* taught by professionals, but just some high school kids who worked at The Y. They were just out to make a quick buck from the parents, YMCA sponsored and all.

The first thing this tall, geeky-looking, nerd-boarder told me about was a kickflip.

"Okay, Carl. So here's the deal. You got a kick-flip, here." He stood on his board, directly in front of me. "Here, I'll show you a thing or— Wait. Stand back, bro."

So I did. Geeky was regular footed, so he had his right foot on the tail of the board, and his left foot was toward the middle, both wobbling to crap. Then he snapped the tail with his right foot, slid his left foot up at an angle, and knocked the board over in a barrel roll of one spin, then landed.

"See, Carl? See? That's a kickflip."

"Cool," I said. "I can't wait to do that."

• • •

A few days later, some time after school, I was at The Y with the geek-trainer. He was showing me a few things. We were not inside the park, per se, but just at the basketball court, behind the pavilion looking out toward the park. It was like being dick-teased, except I was nine so I didn't really know the feeling just yet.

There was a lone ramp right-centered on the court. Geeky was teaching me about just plain old riding down the thing.

"Okay, Carl, now listen. You listenin'?"

I nodded. "Yup."

"Okay. So. You gotta stand up on top of this ramp." He was tall, so he picked me up and placed me on top of the ramp, then put my Walmart board under me. "There . . . we . . . ah, *go*. Okay, now then. Stand up straight. That's right, that's right. Okay. Now what you got to do is pump."

"Pump?" I said.

"Yes. *Pump*. You have to lean down onto the ramp, not just stand up straight and ride down it. . . . PUMP!"

So I laughed, and tried to "pump."

The first try went like this: I push a little bit passed the start of the ramp's incline, then jumped back and my board flew down the ramp, and I was left standing there where I started. I felt really shameful at the fact that I may, or may not, get this down right.

"You can't be scared, Carl," Geeky said. "Listen. This is not something easy, but trust me you have to get over fear."

Get over fear. That was something I'd never done. "Okay," I said. "But it looks so scary!"

"It is, Carl. Try again."

"Okay."

So I tried again.

The second try went like this: I took one look down the ramp, took a deep breath, relaxed, tried to embrace the idea, and then took a small, slow push. The back two wheels passed the start of the incline. I skidded and wobbled and fell on my ass, sliding down the small four-foot ramp. I felt better about that try, like I could really actually land it.

"That's good," Geeky said. "Try again?"

Normally, I would have cried but this time I didn't. I said to Geeky, "Yes," and nodded.

The third try went like this: I rolled down the ramp, got two-feet on flat, skidded, fell.

"Better," Geeky said. And then he gave me a high-five. "Much, much better, bro."

I learned that if you tried long enough, you'd make the trick.

The next time I saw Geeky at The Y, I finally rolled down that ramp, in style. I cheered. My mother saw, and she cheered. We bought ice cream after. I never attended another lesson after that.

· · ·

The trailer I lived in was small, but outside was a completely foreign to me because I was so young and outside was like the equivalent of doing something the "big kids" did. I would skittishly walk out front, board in hand, and try to do pushes on the flat asphalt a few times. Nothing was like it. The wind in my face; the feeling of gliding; the feeling of flying. But the craziest part was that I spent so much time out front of my house, I eventually I got sick of looking at the same old pebbles on the asphalt. I needed OUT. I needed to FLY.

So I went a few feet down, a few feet more, closer, closer closer. Until finally I was on the main roadway, six houses down from mine. The roadway was always empty. On that corner, though, was a little Mexican boy. His name was Ray.

I was back to being that elementary school type of bashful, as lame as that sounds. Ray was there, but we never spoke. He was only three houses down from the corner of the main road, just skateboarding, doing the very thing I was doing. I had to introduce myself. So I rolled on over to him.

"Hey," I said him.

"Hey!"

"Wanna play S.K.A.T.E.?"

"Huh?"

"SKATE!"

"Oh yeah. Sure," he said.

We were kidding ourselves. I had seen him skate before. He could barely ollie. So what we did was basically just ride into the grass and get a certain distance. If you got passed the person, you got a letter. We may have gotten about eight or nine feet at the most. I forget who won.

"What's your name?" the kid asked me.

"Carl. What's yours?"

"Ray."

This was how I met my first skater buddy.

• • •

Everyday Ray was at my house. He was an annoying little nerd-boarder, but was so passionate about his skateboarding, like how I was. He told me he had another friend the next street over that was his buddy that skateboarded too.

"Cool," I said with fake indifference.

"Wanna meet him?" Ray asked.

"Yes."

It was a Saturday. Why not?

• • •

The kid's house was just like mine, only dirty as hell. He was a red-haired, lanky, twelve years old, and flea-infested from head to toe. Literally, one second he's talking and the next second you got a flea on your arm. He was a good kid though. He was sweet and wouldn't hurt anybody. He liked snakes too. A snake fanatic in fact.

Ray knocked on the kid's door. The kid swung the door open, stared at us both, then walked back inside his dark house.

"Come on," Ray said, looking over at me.

I was sketched out. Ray and I walked in. The first thing I smelled was something like wood chips and poop, and the ground was sticky and black. Food was on tables. Dishes weren't done. A pigsty. "Come check out this new game I got, bro!" this dirty kid said to Ray from his couch in the living room.

"Oh shit, it's the new *Tony Hawk Pro Skater*. Is that number three?"

"Yeah, bro . . ."

"What's Tony Hawk?" I said.

The two of them looked at me, looked at themselves, then rolled their heads back and howled with laughter.

"What's so funny?" I asked them.

"Nothing," Ray said, still sort of laughing. "It's just . . . well, um . . . in skateboarding he's like the most famous dude."

"So . . . ?"

"And that's it."

"I think it's better if you just play it, man," the dirty-kid said. "What's your name, by the way?"

Back in those days, introductions didn't matter until it was time to actually *have to* introduce. We were kids, you see. Little pricks.

"Carl," I said. "Yours?"

He said that his name was Stephen, and then handed me the controller. I played that thing for the next three hours, hogging the thing. Ray and Stephen got pissed that they couldn't get a turn. They skated outside, finally, after admitting defeat.

•   •   •

The next day Stephen and Ray knocked on my house's sliding-glass door, eager and waiting. I was just waking up and putting my shoes on. I kind of didn't want to see either of them, but I guess it's always nice to see people even if you don't really want to. The only reason why I didn't is because I thought they were immature and annoying. All skateboys are immature and annoying, including me.

I went up to that sliding glass door, picked up the wooden blocker from its latch, slid the door over and asked them: "What?"

"Carl!" said Ray, immediately coming in, Stephen followed suit, "there's something crazy happening!"

"What?"

Stephen butted in: "The Y, they are having a contest. It's the Etnies contest."

"Cool," I said. "What do you do there?"

"Watch," Ray said.

"Do they have food?"

"Do you really care about food, man?"

I shrugged.

"Lets just go," Ray said. "My mother is outside, man. Come on!"

"Oh, all right," I said and got a move on.

•   •   •

I didn't bring my board to The Y since Ray and Stephen told me we were "just watching." It was weird because there was a huge crowd there. I guess I never heard of a "contest" until now.

This projector was playing under the pavilion while we waited for the show to start. It played some very old, very crappy skate video, but I didn't judge it like that at the time. I remember some guy did a manual—that's where a guy balances on just the back wheels—and he did it on one wheel. I thought that was insane. The crowd screamed wildly.

For a second I was confused and I didn't know why. It was probably because I didn't understand the concept of tricks. So, after the video was done I got up and then, for the first time, went out into the park, where all the pros in the video I saw were congregated.

There were so many of them—all doing flips and tricks in every direction. One moment, they were launching five-feet in the air and landing on a plastic barrier, and the next, they were doing twists on the hip ramp. I was in the love with the idea; I always was creative, so therefore, I wanted to experiment and create new, exciting tricks, just like those pros did. My friends were next to me viewing this in awe; they hadn't realized what had sparked inside me, this explosion to make and create this fine, beautiful work of art.

• • •

If I wasn't at school, I was skating the front of my house. I didn't play many video games anymore on the Nintendo 64. All I wanted to do was skate. Even when Ray and Stephen would come over to skate, they would get tired of it by eight o'clock and go home; meanwhile I stayed out. My mother noticed the obsession. I would skip out on dinner sometimes. My mother liked the idea that I was getting interested in something, but she didn't like the idea that it was consuming me. She also didn't like the fact that she was spending so much money buying me shoes which only lasted for about three weeks and then, *poof!* they would become shredded and unusable. I had no clue. I didn't know what money was. Boy, what an odd thing now, looking back. Not knowing what money was.

• • •

My father was supposed to pick me up this one Saturday. He drove a Ford F-150. The guy did screen enclosures and his company was called "The Screen Guy." That's it. There was vinyl on the side of his truck, showing this. My father had many employees, but not enough work. The guy smoked four packs of cigarettes and drank one case of beer a day.

Sometimes scotch when he had the money. Mostly Budweiser though. I hated that he drank so much, and I didn't want to be around it, but, by proxy, he was my dad and I was his son and so in order to see him I had to suck it up and deal with it.

He called my mother when I got up, which was nine a.m. He told her that he would be there at two o'clock to pick me up. He told me that he wanted to take me to the water park near his house in Stuart, Florida, which was one hour north.

"Carl has started a new hobby, Stephen," my mother said. His name was Stephen, just like Ray's friend.

"Oh. Is that right?" I imagined him saying. I never heard the other end of the line, ever. I'm glad I didn't.

"Please be here at two, Stephen," my mother said. "I mean it. And please, for the love of—"

Then she stopped. I heard growling and yelling from the microphone of our house phone, and shortly after my mother would hang up. Then she came up to me in the living room as I was eating a bowl of cereal she made for me.

"Your father is going to be coming down at two o'clock, Carl."

"Is he?"

"I hope so."

"I hope so, too."

"But for the love of God, just go skate with your friends until then. Come back and two, son."

"Yeah, Mom."

"Love you."

"You always say that."

"What?"

"Nothing," I said.

(My father never asked what my hobby was.)

I was skating with Ray and Stephen outside Stephen's house when two o'clock came.

"Guys," I said. "Watch this!"

I pushed, pushed, pushed as hard as I could—then KICKED my board toward a trash can. *Slam!*

Stephen goes, "*Shit* man! What the heck! That was my cousin's house! My fuckin' *uncle's* house!"

"I didn't know," I said. "Is he going to notice?"

"Most likely," he laughed passively. "I mean, look at the dent on that hoe."

He wasn't kidding. The dent was gnar-kill. A steel trash can. "Oh," I said, "well, um, I gotta go anyway guys."

"Okay, kid . . ." Stephen said, "but if my uncle asks, I'm saying *you* did it. I don't want that guy on my ass. Forget that shit."

Ray laughed.

"I gotta go," I said. I wanted to get out of there as soon as possible because the thought of getting into trouble was too much for me. So I left, heading home.

• • •

It was 2:30 p.m. when I finally got home. My mother didn't even get mad at me, mostly because (a) My father wasn't there, and (b) She was tanning. She was always tanning. That, or doing lawn work. We had the best lawn, I remember that clearly.

I was playing video games with my legs crossed on the carpet when I heard my mother obviously on the phone with my father.

"Stephen, I swear to God. . . . He's your *son*. . . . Where are you?! This is messed up, Stephen. . . . I do NOT want to hear it from you . . . For God's sake, he's your *son!* . . . You know what . . . No! Forget it. Bye," and she hung up.

Then she came into the living room from the dining room and told me the gist of it.

"Dad isn't coming, honey."

"Why?" I asked.

"He's . . ."—she didn't want to say it—"working."

If I was the version of myself today, I would have said: "Typical," and continued on with my life, but I was only nine so I said, "Okay, Mom. It's okay."

I could tell my mother was about to cry.

• • •

I left the house once I knew my father wasn't coming. It was that way. My father was a drunk, and he was probably drinking and forgot to pick me up. He was a relaxed son of a bitch, but oh well, what was I to do about that? I left, that's what.

I went back to Ray and Stephen, in front of Stephen's house. They were still there but they weren't skating. They were in front of some house close by, talking to some older guy.

I rolled up on my board and stood there listening to them talking.

"Yeah, man, the news is pretty crazy nowadays," the old guy was saying.

"Really? Pops says those guys are loaded," Stephen said.

Ray was just standing there.

"Absolutely," the old guy answered, "it's nothing but a bunch of rich morons lookin' to scare you. I don't watch it no more, except for the hurricanes obviously." He sucked in his nose, hawked up something in his throat, and spat on the asphalt. Then he looked at me: "Who's this kid?"

"Oh," said Ray, "that's just Carl."

"Is he the kid that hit my trashcan?"

"Ah . . ." Stephen hesitated. "I don't kn—"

"Don't pull a fast one on me, Stephen. He has trouble written all over him. Look at him. Looks like a damn thug."

The old guy left after saying that, and went back under his archway, closing the gate behind him. To the left and right eight-foot tall, perfectly cut, bushes circled his entire house. His lawn was a lot better than my mother's, which was hard to top.

"Is he mad at me?" I asked Ray and Stephen.

They shrugged.

• • • •

Next weekend my father flaked out again. It was a recurring thing. First, Mom would give a time. Second, Mom would call, call, call, and get a run-around. It was like going insane. So, in the kitchen, finally, I laid it down for her real sweet as she was chopping some vegetables.

"Mom, he's not coming. Can I skate with my friends?"

"Honey, it's getting dark."

"It's only six."

"I know, but—"

"PLEASE!" I shouted.

My mother was startled. "Carl, don't you EVER do that again, you hear me?"

I nodded.

My mother continued, "You can go. But be back around dinnertime. Your father isn't coming, but I want you to be here for the food I cook. Okay? Please don't be late, and please, please, *please* be safe."

I nodded. Then I left the room, went into the dining room, grabbing my board. I came back into the kitchen.

"Mom?"

She turned around over her shoulder. "Yes?"

"Do I look like a thug?" I asked her.

"No, son. No. You don't. You look like an angel."

"Oh," I said, then left my house.

•　•　•

For the longest time I've had the fondest memories of Donald. He was probably one of my best friends. He was taller, muscular, slimmer, thirteen years old, had black straight hair that draped perfectly over his forehead and ears, and he was always talking about chicks. Chicks were always the thing, I remember. It was all we talked about. He was also the son to the guy whose trashcan I damaged.

I was skating down my street cutting the corner left, skating about another block down, cutting a corner left again, and then seeing Stephen and some kid—no, it was Ray.

I was sort of tiptoeing my pushes down the street. "Who is that?" I said to myself.

As I got up to the two of them, "and this chick was grinding on my lap," was said by this kid, Donald. "She just kept going."

"Really?" said Stephen. He was laughing. "Man, what's her name?"

"Kat. It's really 'Katherine,' but I call her Kat. Everyone does."

"Hey guys," I little kid'd, my voice all high-pitched. "What's going on?"

"Who's this?" Donald asked Stephen.

"He's this kid that skates with Ray."

"Ah. Cool. Hey, kid. What's your name?"

I said, "Carl."

"Cool, man. Ever heard of the cop joke?"

I shook my head.

And Donald said: "Really? Never?" He looked at Stephen who was laughing. "Okay, so it starts like this: This guy is driving his car down the highway. Going *fast* man. I'm the guy. Then I see these cops right in my rearview. So I pull over. I wasn't scared or nothin'—yeah. Anyway, I pull over, look in my rearview, and this girl cop is walking from her car."

"You forgot the other guy," Stephen corrected.

"Oh yeah. Thanks. So anyway, it's this guy, Stephen, and another guy next to him. That's you, Carl. It's all three of us in the car. So the girl cop comes up to me and I roll down my window. The girl cop goes, 'License and Registration.' So I hand her it, she looks. Then she says, 'You guys were going fast, but I'll make a deal with you.' So of course we all nod or whatever. The girl cop goes, 'Show me your cocks. If you are passed two-inches you don't get a ticket, Mr. Donald.' We all shrug and we start pulling our cocks out. The girl cop goes to me: nine inches. She goes to Stephen: eh . . . six inches. Then she goes to you, Carl: one and a half inches!"

Stephen was laughing like crazy.

Then Donald says, "The girl cop says, 'Close enough,' and walks away. We drive off. And then, get this: you say, 'Good thing I popped a boner.'"

I never saw two guys laugh as hard as they did in my life. They we leaning over touching their knees and shit.

Then I ask them: "What's a boner?"

Donald and Stephen stop laughing and Donald asks me, "You really don't know what a boner is?"

"No."

Then they really started laughing even more.

• • •

Later, Donald brought over what he called *The Shreder Sheder Video*. We watched it. I saw Bradley Kromer, Toaster, Sam Burgeon, Mark Turner, Charles Leslee, and a bunch of other dudes in there. They all killed it! I was so inspired! The intro to the video played a song call "Brand New Colony," by The Postal Service. To this day I still listen to that song and smile.

late-2001

I hadn't seen my dad in close to four weeks. I was missing him. I always missed him, even though we never did anything whenever I *did* see him. I'm not sure why. He was always so nice to me. He was a good dad, in that way. My mother was really trying to get him to show up that weekend, which was another Saturday.

It was six o'clock and I found my way to front of Stephen's house, which was three trailers down from Donald's house. Donald and Stephen were there; and Ray was there too. They were all just skating out front Donald's house. I rode up.

"Hey, dudes!" I said.

Nobody looked up. So I skated up to them; they were skating flat-ground (meaning that there wasn't a decline or incline, just flatness), doing flip tricks. Donald was good. He was doing kickflips; and he did them with style, better than Geeky at The Y.

Donald landed a kickflip and rode right into me. "Woah! Hey, Carl. What's up, lil' man," he said.

"What's up?"

"I heard you were the one that fucked my trash can up."

I didn't say anything.

"Nice shirt," Donald said.

"My mother bought it," I told him. "My dad is coming and she wanted me to look nice. I can't skate as hard or fall because it will make the shirt dirty."

"*Ooooooh!*" Donald said with his eyes big. "I see! Well! How about we do this!" and he grabbed me by the shoulders—it was almost as if that was queue for Ray and Stephen to help him, because then they came over and grabbed each of my feet. I started to scream.

"NO! NO! STOP!"

They were picking me up and walking we over to the trashcan that was at the end of Donald's driveway.

"My dad beat my ass for you bending this shit," Donald was saying. "He had to buy a new one, kid. I gotta teach you a lesson." He was saying this calmly, as if it wasn't a big deal. "We have arrived."

I looked over my shoulder, toward the ground. What came into my visuals: the asphalt's shells blurring diagonally, then the open container of the trashcan. I could see little flies circling around in there.

"STOP! I DIDN'T MEAN TO DO IT! STOP!" My voice was cracking.

"Too late, Carl," Donald said. Then all three of them dropped me inside the trashcan, where I felt something mush under my shoes. It stunk immediately.

I started crying.

"WHY?! NO FAIR! WHY! WHY DID YOU GUYS DO THAT?! I DIDN'T MEAN TO MESS UP YOUR TRASHCAN! NOW MY DAD'S GOING TO *KILL* ME! I STINK!"

Ray, Stephen, and Donald were all laughing. Donald said, "Maybe next time you'll know better, won't you?"

I wiggled and the can toppled over with me still inside it. The can dropped. Stinky water was pouring out of it and lapping out onto the ground, like guts. I squirmed out of the trashcan, stood up, and grabbed my board. I heard Ray, Stephen and Donald laughing as I sped home, crying.

•   •   •

My mother immediately noticed the smell.

"Carl! You're filthy!"

"I'm sorry, Mom." I truly was. "My friends dropped me into a trashcan."

"That's awful! I'm going to have a talk with their parents, you just wait and see!"

"NO, MOM! DON'T!"

"Why would they do that?!"

"I dented their trashcan."

She gasped.

"Young man!"

I frowned with my head down.

"Sorry, Mom."

• • •

About thirty-four minutes later my father showed up, drunk. He rolled up in his truck and had his flood-lights on. We immediately knew he was home because our house was made of this really crappy aluminum and was sort of see through, so the lights would brighten the house a bit. Not to mention his truck was messed up and made lots of noise.

My mother and I walked out front. It was dark outside but I remember seeing my father climb out of his car, beer cans flooding out, and him closing the door. He walked up to us and reeked of beer and stale cigarette. His belly was popping out of his shirt. He looked, smelled, and acted like hell.

"Sorry I'm late," he laughed.

"Can always count on you, Stephen."

He laughed again, and then kneeled down to me. "Hey, buddy. You ready?"

I nodded.

"You're not taking him like that," my mother said. "Hell no."

He looked up. "You don't tell me what to do with my boy!"

"You're drunk, Stephen."

"No I'm not. I'm buzzed. It's not a big deal. I can drive."

"You're NOT taking your son like this!"

"Watch me," he said. Then he grabbed hold of my arm and started tugging me. "Come on, son. Come."

I was getting scared but I hadn't seen my dad so I wanted to hang with him, it was such a long time since I had done that.

"NO, Stephen!" my mother was saying. She was pulling his shirt. "STOP! KIDNAPPER!"

He shrugged her off. "Get off of me."

I remember my father opened his truck's door and threw me in. He told me, "Hop over to the passenger side, will ya, buddy?"

So I did.

He got in, and I saw my mother tugging some more at his shirt. He shut the door. I was hearing, "MY BABY! MY BABY!" from my mother outside the car. The windows were up so I couldn't hear it too well.

My father put the car in reverse, put his head behind my seat's headrest, looked back, and reversed out of my mother's driveway. She was screaming and screaming and screaming.

"I'M CALLING THE POLICE, STEPHEN! I SWEAR!"

He grinned. By that time, we were already out on the street. He rolled down his window. "He'll be back tomorrow." He blew a kiss. "Bye, Kay!"

"YOU ASSHOLE, STEPHEN!"

We sped off.

•　　•　　•

It was raining and it was dark inside my dad's truck. The rain was so heavy that all you saw was the glass and the beads of water smacking down. My father didn't have the radio on for some odd reason. I think he liked the rain or something.

"Dad?"

"Yeah, buddy. What?"

"How can you see in this?"

He pointed his index with his hand still gripping the steering wheel. He said, "The lines. The headlights light up the lines on the streets. That's what you look at."

"But, Dad, how can you see cars in front of you or to the side of you?"

He laughed. "You don't. You just hope they aren't there."

I looked out the window and notice my shirt smelled horrible. My father never commented on it.

*   *   *

After getting to his house though, he crashed out. It was only eleven o'clock. He was on the sofa and passed out to *Wheel of Fortune* on the TV. Before that he was watching the Sci-Fi channel. What was playing was this weird space odyssey. He was always either watching that or soft-core porn. There was always a beer in his hand. His eyes never left the TV. If he wasn't doing that, he was playing *Starcraft* on the computer. His leg always shook whenever he played the game. He never answered to his name. You had to repeat "Stephen!" about twenty times before he would snap out of his gamer trance and look at you. That night when he was sleeping, someone knocked on the door. There were flashlights moving side to side and up and down through the window. I answered it. It was two police officers dressed in blue.

"Hi, sonny," one of them said. "Excuse me. Grab him, Jon."

Jon took hold of my arm. I saw the other cop walk through the house and into the living room where my dad was asleep on the sofa. He poked him with the flashlight. "Stephen Klitz," he told him. "You're under arrest."

He was snoring away.

I'm not sure what happened after that because there were two cars and I went inside one with Jon and was drove home, back to my mother's house. He asked why I smelled bad and if my mother neglects me too.

early-2002

Two weeks later at Boy Scouts, my mother met a guy named Chaz. They started dating and I became good friends with his sons, CJ and Shawn. Eventually I was just going to Chaz's house with my mother after school. CJ was the cool one, Shawn was the youngin'. I was a year older than CJ. Shawn was three or so years younger.

Kingdom Hearts, a video game by Square Enix and Disney, came out and was the highest-selling game on the market. Mainly because it was a platform game with a mixture of all the famous Disney characters and their worlds, plus all the excitement and style of the *Final Fantasy* franchise. My mother bought it three months after the release because she didn't have the money when I asked for it. That's why I was over CJ and Shawn's house. My mother didn't mind because she was having sex with the dad, I guess. But I don't want to be crude so . . . "making love."

* * *

Report cards for the quarter came, which was shitty for me because my mother grabbed the mail from her P.O. box before we drove to Chaz's one day.

"Oh look, Carl. Reee*port* card!"

I buried my face in my hands.

* * *

We got to Chaz's house and there he was: Chaz, sitting on his porch and smoking a cigarette in one hand and sipping beer in the other. He stood up when my mother and me walked up.

"Hey, my fine piece of ass!"

"Hey, Chaz." My mother blushed.

They embraced, kissed, all that. Afterward, my mother asked, "Did Shawn and Chaz" (meaning CJ) "get their report cards?"

"Oh yeah!" Chaz said. "They did. Shawn's actually in his room right now. He got all *C's* and a *D*."

"What'd CJ get?" my mother asked.

"All A's."

"Of course."

"What'd Carl get?" Chaz said like I wasn't there.

"Don't know. Haven't looked," my mother said.

Then Chaz sort of looked over her shoulder and said, "*OoooOooooo* troubleeeeee!"

That's when I knew I hated him.

* * *

In the kitchen, Chaz had finished making steaks. He was always making steak and potatoes, which was odd because he was obviously an Italian man. Fat. Big gut. Beer-drinker. Ass-hat.

"Kids! CJ! Shawn! Dinner's ready!" Chaz shouted. Then, to my mother, "You want a big steak or a little one?"

"No thanks. I'm fine." She set the report card down on the table. "Should we open up Carl's grades or something? I don't know."

NOTES

NOTES

NOTES

NOTES